ECONOMIC DEVELOPMENT AND MENTAL ILLNESS

Social, economic, and technological changes disrupt many Indigenous, ethnic, and rural communities even when offering progress. Under these conditions, social and psychological dysfunctions are likely to emerge. This book provides insights regarding how to anticipate, prevent, and, when necessary, provide mitigation strategies to communities and individuals who suffer as a result.

This book, the first of its kind, provides an overview of strategic and policy issues involving the relationship between change and dysfunction, enabling the reader to more effectively deal with potentially hurtful influences in proactive, equitable, and culturally sensitive ways. After providing a theoretical overview, methods for anticipating the hurtful impacts of change are discussed, along with techniques for mitigating its negative effects upon communities and individuals.

Learning objectives and discussion questions are included with each chapter, and the book can serve as a text for courses on indigenous economic development, Native studies, culturally appropriate business, and culturally competent therapy. It can also be used as a professional handbook for practitioners working with communities affected by these issues.

Alf H. Walle is a former professor of Tribal Management, and also directed a residential facility serving Indigenous alcoholics. Focusing on change, disruption, dysfunction, and therapy, Walle combines academic and practitioner orientations.

ECONOMIC DEVELOPMENT AND MENTAL ILLNESS

Anticipating and Mitigating Disruptive Change

Alf H. Walle

LONDON AND NEW YORK

First published 2020
by Routledge
2 Park Square, Milton Park, Abingdon, Oxon OX14 4RN

and by Routledge
52 Vanderbilt Avenue, New York, NY 10017

Routledge is an imprint of the Taylor & Francis Group, an informa business

© 2020 Alf H. Walle

The right of Alf H. Walle to be identified as author of this work has been asserted by him in accordance with sections 77 and 78 of the Copyright, Designs and Patents Act 1988.

All rights reserved. No part of this book may be reprinted or reproduced or utilised in any form or by any electronic, mechanical, or other means, now known or hereafter invented, including photocopying and recording, or in any information storage or retrieval system, without permission in writing from the publishers.

Trademark notice: Product or corporate names may be trademarks or registered trademarks, and are used only for identification and explanation without intent to infringe.

British Library Cataloguing-in-Publication Data
A catalogue record for this book is available from the British Library

Library of Congress Cataloging-in-Publication Data
Names: Walle, Alf H., author.
Title: Economic development and mental illness : anticipating and mitigating disruptive change / Alf H. Walle.
Description: Abingdon, Oxon ; New York, NY : Routledge, 2020. | Includes bibliographical references and index.
Identifiers: LCCN 2019037220 (print) | LCCN 2019037221 (ebook) | ISBN 9780367278441 (hbk) | ISBN 9780367278458 (pbk) | ISBN 9780429298240 (ebk)
Subjects: LCSH: Anomy. | Economic development—Psychological aspects. | Mental health—Economic aspects.
Classification: LCC HM816 .W35 2020 (print) | LCC HM816 (ebook) | DDC 338.9—dc23
LC record available at https://lccn.loc.gov/2019037220
LC ebook record available at https://lccn.loc.gov/2019037221

ISBN: 978-0-367-27844-1 (hbk)
ISBN: 978-0-367-27845-8 (pbk)
ISBN: 978-0-429-29824-0 (ebk)

Typeset in Bembo
by Apex CoVantage, LLC

 Printed in the United Kingdom by Henry Ling Limited

Alf Julius Walle, my grandfather, died in his 80s in Manistee, Michigan, USA (a town on Lake Michigan with a large population of Norwegian immigrants and those who descend from them). After death, arrangements for the funeral service were drawn up. The family requested that an old Lutheran Pastor, long retired, preside.

The current minister, a young man who spoke perfect English and was college educated, said that was impossible because the elderly man was no longer ordained. We were told that the Lutherans (at least in Michigan) had taken steps to reduce the ethnic flavor of congregations that had originally served immigrant groups. As a result, reverends with strong Norwegian accents, who were attuned to the Old World, had been cast aside and replaced with young Americans who had completed seminary in the United States.

At the family's insistence, however, the old man was given permission to speak as a guest, although the prayers and other "Godly stuff" had to be performed by an active member of the clergy. When giving his eulogy, this son of Norway made a strange statement for a man of the cloth when he observed, with a strong accent (almost broken English), that "Thor has taken his last apprentice home". The young minister was shocked that a pagan god had been celebrated at a Christian funeral.

The pagan reference had been made because my grandfather was a blacksmith and Thor is the God of Iron. Although religion has its place, so does ethnic identity. And Thor continues to be a Scandinavian hero, not just a rival god. Although the Christian minister was appalled, the family was most appreciative of those words. I remember them to this day.

Besides being a blacksmith (who worked as a welder at a local salt mine), family lore recalls that my grandfather had an informal role as a "lay preacher" who long worked with the local church to help people adjust and cope. In this role, he did not baptize or carry the word of God. Instead, he helped people adjust to life in the New World. If people missed their home, he would go over for a cup of coffee and talk of the fjords in Norwegian. Doing so often helped to control the sadness and pain. This was an important role because many people became despondent when far from their old beloved homelands. My grandfather helped these displaced souls to cope and adjust.

As the Lutheran denomination struggled to become more generic and non-ethnic in flavor and appearance, this culturally sensitive role of the church seems to have been discarded, but for many years it served well.

I guess you could say that my grandfather was, in his own intuitive way, a culturally aware therapist who understood that people subjected to cultural change and loss often need help adjusting. Today that need continues in many places. Not among Norwegian-Americans, perhaps, but clearly among other groups facing the pain and stress of change and cultural losses. This book deals with such circumstances. In particular, indigenous, ethnic, and traditional peoples who are experiencing social and economic transformations are often alienated and befuddled by change and loss. They need culturally tailored interventions to help them deal with these realities.

This book is dedicated to my grandfather and to all others who help people cope as they face cultural change and loss.

CONTENTS

Preface	*ix*

SECTION 1
A social background   **1**

Prologue to Section 1	3
1 What is anomie?	5
2 Coping with anomie	17
3 Hurtful impacts of anomie	26
4 Positive responses to anomie	35
5 Effected communities	46
Epilogue to Section 1	56

SECTION 2
Psychological perspectives   **57**

Prologue to Section 2	59
6 The standard anomie model	61

viii Contents

7	Implications of cultural trauma	75
8	Terror Management Theory	90
	Epilogue to Section 2	106

SECTION 3
Strategies of mitigation   **109**

	Prologue to Section 3	111
9	Client-centered therapy	113
10	Representative tactics	132
	Epilogue to Section 3	148

Final words   *150*
Index   *152*

PREFACE

Today, many parts of the world are experiencing an unprecedented level of economic development and social engineering. Due to such initiatives, the people who live in these regions often experience increased contact with the outside world, coupled with pressures to change. Numerous positive advances result from these relationships and the opportunities they bring.

The benefits gained, unfortunately, are often simultaneously associated with hurtful side effects. The legacy of colonialism and neo-colonialism, for example, provides many examples of this possibility. Particularly significant is the tendency for local cultures, communities, and peoples to experience unprecedented burdens, stresses, and strains that undercut their heritage and way of life. The resulting social and psychological assaults can lead to emotional trauma and psychological dysfunction at both the individual and the community levels.

These hurtful potentials need to be anticipated and combated in a preemptive manner. The most effective response is to envision potential problems and pressures as a first step in devising strategies for preventing or mitigating their damaging influences. Sadly, on many occasions, plans to do so are merely envisioned after the fact, and/or are not developed in a forward-looking, proactive manner.

The goal of this volume is to provide a useful orientation for people who deal with economic development within rural regions and among ethnic enclaves (which may or may not be indigenous in nature). The text is divided into three sections: (1) "A social background" introduces and explores the concept of anomie, a response to profound and disruptive and social change; (2) "Psychological perspectives" examines a representative array of models that portray how mental health can be impacted by these changes; and (3) "Strategies of mitigation" explores ways to lessen the negative consequences of social and economic development. My goal is to help all interested parties (including those impacted, counselors

x Preface

and therapists who help them, as well as economic development specialists who bring disruptive transformations) to better envision ways for people to benefit from social and economic development without being hurt in the process.

Section 1 introduces a theoretical background. Chapter 1 explores how rapid social change can transform people's lives and, in the process, trigger psychological dysfunction. In the late 19th century, French anthropologist Emile Durkheim compared small, intimate social groups with those who live urban lives that are typified by detached relationships with others. Durkheim found that those who abandoned their intimate rural relationships and migrated to impersonal cities were likely to suffer emotionally and psychologically. Although Durkheim work is monumental, he failed to explore the full range of reactions that result from profound change.

In Chapter 2, Durkheim's theories of change and dysfunction are expanded by analyzing the work of American sociologist Robert Merton, who observed that some reactions to anomie are hurtful while others are positive and productive. Merton, however, dealt with homogeneous cultures in which most people embrace similar beliefs, desires, and attitudes. To deal with distinctive peoples, cultures, and societies, Merton's work needs to be adjusted with an eye towards local distinctiveness.

The next two chapters focus upon specific case studies. Chapter 3 provides examples of hurtful and dysfunctional responses to anomie and social change while Chapter 4 demonstrates that under some conditions the results can be positive and productive.

Chapter 5 completes Section 1 by analyzing a range of social groups including indigenous, ethnic, and traditional cultures that live in a variety of settings including "third world" and "fourth world" environments. The basic premise is that under certain circumstances, specific people with particular backgrounds are likely to respond to change in predictable ways that can be anticipated. By understanding these predictable potentials, choosing proactive and beneficial strategies can be more easily accomplished.

Section 2, "Psychological perspectives", introduces a variety of methods that can be used when analyzing and responding to dysfunction caused by contact with the dominant outside world. These discussions are not exhaustive; they merely introduce representative techniques for dealing with dysfunction that can result from unmitigated change wrought by powerful outside forces. Chapter 6 more fully develops the concept of anomie discussed in Section 1 in order to demonstrate its therapeutic value. Chapter 7 continues by presenting additional representative methods for dealing with dysfunction that is triggered by economic development and social change. Revolving around cultural trauma, the basic premise is that unmitigated economic development and social change can cause people to suffer. The memories of these hurtful consequences often trigger trauma that is capable of generating dysfunction in individuals. Beginning with an analysis of PTSD and continuing with discussions of trauma initiatives by SAMHSA, theories of trauma are adapted to deal with dysfunction caused by cultural change and economic interventions.

This generic discussion is followed by Chapter 8, which deals with an innovative branch of psychology known as Terror Management. This emerging school of thought suggests that people tend to be preoccupied with their death (or at least a fate that is analogous to it). Individuals, furthermore, often identify with their community, culture, and way of life, viewing it as an extension of themselves. As a result, a strong and functioning heritage can provide comfort and security by affirming that their heritage is immortal and will live on after they die. The comfort provided by this knowledge can help prevent dysfunction. If the culture is weak, undercut, or in a state of disarray, however, this security can be stripped away, leading to a greater level of dysfunction within the community and among individuals.

The final section of the book deals with "Strategies of mitigation". The goal is to chart a broad course that helps people deal with (if not proactively prevent) dysfunction associated with economic development and other aspects of cultural and social change. As with Section 2, the discussions are suggestive, not exhaustive.

Chapter 9 emphasizes that evaluating and treating clients on their own terms is vital. To do so, those who provide services need to understand the people they serve and treat them in an appropriate and culturally sensitive manner. The Cultural Safety movement, originating in New Zealand and rapidly expanding elsewhere, is a product of the indigenous Maori people and can be viewed as a positive aspect of their cultural renaissance. The Cultural Competence movement, in contrast, is largely the product of counselors and health care providers who seek the ability to deal with other peoples in a respectful, appropriate, and effective manner. Both of these approaches, in their own ways, seek to provide clients and their cultures with parity, equity, and self-determinism within the context of healing.

Having reviewed these movements, a variety of specific techniques are discussed. Carl Rogers' work advocates "client-centered" therapy that is largely directed by the clients who receive services. Although beneficial, allowing such freedom can result in a lack of direction and, thereby, fail to address specific problems. A useful alternative involves using semi-directed methods, such as Motivational Interviewing, in which clients are given a level of control within a loose structure that is provided by the therapeutic relationship. In both cases, benefits can arise when therapists or counselors gain an understanding of their clients and give them a degree of control over the therapeutic relationship. Client input can be especially important where significant cultural and/or social distances exist.

Chapter 10 discusses methods of evaluation and intervention that are representative of culturally competent and client-centered approaches. The work of Gregory Bateson deals with power shifts that often occur when particular people lose or gain clout and effectiveness. This situation can trigger conflict if those who lost respect regroup and seek to reassert their legitimate positions of authority. Although Bateson developed his theory to deal with families impacted by

xii Preface

substance abuse, it can be expanded to deal with others who lose power and authority for any reason, including social and economic transformations.

René Girard believed that much of the tension in the world results from a particular form of hurtful copying that he refers to as mimesis. When people copy and imitate each other, they develop parallel needs, wants, and goals. These emerging similarities often result in envy, conflict, and tension. Many of the problems with economic development can be modeled using such an approach. The work of Bateson and Girard demonstrate how existing theories and methods can be adapted for use among indigenous, ethnic, and traditional people.

In today's world of globalization, not only are increased social contacts and economic interrelationships inevitable, they potentially inflict pain and harm and trigger dysfunction. Agents of contact and change need to be aware of these possibilities. In addition, therapists and human services professionals who serve those who are adversely affected by such events need a better understanding regarding how and why dysfunction arises.

Thus, a two-pronged attack is needed: (1) strategic plans should initially be developed with an eye towards possible negative ramifications and how they can be prevented or mitigated. Therapists, furthermore, (2) need the skills required for serving clients after psychological problems and dysfunction arise.

This book focuses thought in this direction.

SECTION 1
A social background

PROLOGUE TO SECTION 1

Economic development and other social interventions profoundly impact people and their way of life. Those who envision and orchestrate such transformations often laud the resulting benefits derived from these changes. A dark side, unfortunately, often accompanies these efforts because the same changes that bring a "better life" can also create pain and sorrow because of the unintended and unanticipated impacts upon the people's, heritage, traditions, and relationships. Although the quest for appropriate and beneficial "progress" is legitimate, hurtful side effects need to be acknowledged and addressed in both preemptive and remedial ways. This book suggests some representative strategies and tactics for doing so.

The concept of anomie deals with the fact that significant change can lead to cultural disruption, individual alienation, and a breaking down of the rules and relationships that people live by. When these destabilizing situations occur, the potential for psychological dysfunction grows even if positive advances simultaneously occur.

After adapting the concept of anomie to deal with ethnic and rural minorities, examples are provided. On many occasions, of course, these developments and their hurtful consequences can be directly connected with the legacy of colonialism and neo-colonialism. This cause and effect relationship is discussed, along with a recognition that the issue of pain caused by change and anomie is broader and deeper than that. Social and psychological problems are likely to arise wherever social and economic transformations are rapid, not adequately anticipated, unmitigated, and so forth. Because discussions of colonialism and neo-colonialism tend to emphasize the evils of foreign domination and exploitation, this focus can easily draw the reader's attention away from a wide variety of other contexts where anomie exerts pressures that cause suffering and dysfunction. The full range of hurtful influences, of course, needs to be considered.

4 A social background

Section 1 concludes with the discussion of an array of social groups including indigenous, Native, and traditional peoples. This analysis occurs in tandem with an analysis of both Third and Fourth World environments and the roles they often play in fostering psychological dysfunction. Section 1 provides the foundation for a better understanding of how change can lead to dysfunction as well as how these hurtful results can (and should) be addressed in a systematic, appropriate, and culturally sensitive manner.

1

WHAT IS ANOMIE?

Learning objectives

Anomie is a response to rapid change triggered by business activities, governmental policies, cultural change, community pressures, and so forth. After arising, anomie often contributes to social and/or psychological dysfunction. Specifically, this chapter provides insights regarding:

(1) The historic background leading to the concept of anomie.
(2) The influence of the Romantic Era and the Arts and Crafts movement.
(3) Understanding parallels in the work of Tönnies and Durkheim.
(4) Appreciating the work of urban planners, such as Patrick Geddes and Louis Mumford.
(5) Envisioning anomie as a means of understanding cultural stress and pain caused by change.

Introduction

In the 18th and 19th centuries, a transformation began that is typically referred to as the Industrial Revolution (Ashton 1948). An important "first wave" took place in Britain and Continental Europe. During this period, innovations involving mechanization and more rational methods of production transformed society, the workplace, and how people related to each other.

During previous centuries, most people lived within a rural setting and experienced close and responsive contact with nature and each other. Typically, families cultivated small patches of land, growing a significant portion of the food they ate. Intimate social networks existed, allowing people to experience warm, nurturing, and trusting relationships with their neighbors and extended families.

6 A social background

Over time, settlement patterns began to change and economic activities became less based upon face-to-face relationships; increasingly, life became intertwined with (1) powerful outside forces coupled with (2) a dependence upon expensive equipment that local people could not afford. In an earlier era typified by "cottage industries", the work came to where people lived. Now the tables were turned. During the Industrial Revolution, people began relocating to where employment could be found.

A pessimistic picture

Many hurtful events accompanied this change. In 18th-century Britain, for example, small farms were consolidated to provide large stretches of grazing land for sheep. Known as the Highland Clearance (Richards 1982), former tenants who were evicted inevitably migrated to destinations such as Canada or to urban areas within Britain where they survived as best they could. It was a time of sorrow, tension, and uncertainty for rural people who found themselves thrown off the land. A noted novel depicting these events is *Consider the Lilies* by Lain Crichton Smith (1968).

During this period, the protection and comfort previously provided by the local heritage, age-old tradition, and familiar social relationships were stripped away. Under these circumstances, people became increasingly vulnerable to the demands of outsiders and dependent upon performing wage labor. Forced into urban life, hordes of landless refugees no longer had the security of being able to grow their own food. Instead of living in rustic cabins for free, they had to deal with landlords. Without gardens, urban people had to buy food or starve. Life became harsh.

This general scenario had its variants. Nonetheless, throughout 19th-century Europe, distinct but parallel patterns of demographic change swept across the continent, bringing economic vulnerability and social tension. Fear, suffering, and sorrow arose.

Charles Dickens' novels depict the horrific environment caused by that transformation. Writing from personal experience (his father was sent to debtors' prison leading to a precarious existence for young Charles), Dickens arose as a tireless advocate of reform; his writing provides an unflinching portrait of social change, poverty, and the desperation they spawn.

A good example of Dickens' vision is *Oliver Twist*, his second novel, initially published in serial form from 1837 to 1839. Twist, an orphan, begins his struggles in an exploitative workhouse before being apprenticed to an undertaker. Escaping, he ends up in London, meeting a gang of juvenile pickpockets led by Fagin, a well-seasoned professional thief. Twist's adventures extend from there.

In his exposé of urban squalor and exploitation, Dickens provides a graphic portrayal of the life lived by those who were forced to gravitate towards urban centers in the early 19th century. His writing vividly reveals the social problems of his era including child labor, an epidemic of poverty, unsupervised children roaming city streets, and the path to crime awaiting those who were abandoned, hungry, and in need.

An alternative perception

While Dickens was portraying the darker side of urbanization, mechanization, and economic change, the Romantic movement complained about the intellectual framework of and justification for the Industrial Revolution that took many ideas derived from the Enlightenment, a philosophical movement which asserted that science and rational calculation should dominate decisions regarding economics, culture, and society.

The Romantics, in contrast, insisted that the overly rational vision of the Enlightenment was simplistic because it ignored the essence of humanity and the nature of social life. An important component of the Romantic rebuttal is its insistence that emotions, feelings, and relationships (not merely enlightened rational thought) are vital to human nature, social life, and mental health. Although people certainly possess an ability to think and reason, the Romantics affirmed that other equally important aspects of humanity also exist. The passions, arising from temperament, heritage, and circumstance, for example, mold people in distinctive ways. This reality should never be forgotten.

Such Romantic ideas provided the foundation for the Pre-Raphaelites (Bate 1972), an artistic movement that sought to recapture the intimacy of rustic, vernacular life and the creativity arising from it that had existed before the Renaissance. A basic tenet of the Pre-Raphaelites is the belief that the intimate and pastoral lifestyle of earlier times provides the model for a more humane way of life that should replace more modern trends that (in the late 19th century) were transforming domestic life and the workplace.

Using the theories of the Pre-Raphaelites as a foundation, British tastemaker William Morris (Coote 2018) designed and marketed home furnishings that were inspired by the medieval era. This trend in style and fashion has come to be called the Arts and Crafts movement (Naylor 1971). In addition to being a tastemaker, Morris also championed methods of production that provide workers with the social and psychic benefits of handcraftsmanship coupled with intimate, humane relationships with other people. He, in an evangelical manner, advanced the notion that empowering workers and providing a nurturing work environment offered a positive alternative to the slums that surround factories and methods of mass production that chain workers to mind-numbing sweatshops as they make uninspired products of low quality.

A social reformer, Morris wrote a highly regarded utopian novel, *News from Nowhere* (Morris 2003), that depicts a world where assembly lines and cities have been replaced by rustic, rural life, intimate relationships between people, and artistic craftsmanship. According to Morris, such technologies, methods of production, and social relationships would usher in a better life for all.

In America, meanwhile, Elbert Hubbard (Champney 1983) fell under the sway of William Morris' vision of a rustic utopia where people embraced their work

8 A social background

TABLE 1-1 The Arts and Crafts Movement

Topic	Analysis
Basic Description	The Arts and Crafts movement advocated rustic, rural life while emphasizing personal freedom, dignity, and handcraftsmanship. It fueled a major social movement and popularized an important style of architecture, home furnishings, and personal products.
Operational Tactics	Decentralize the organization. Give workers freedom. Create an environment that is close to the earth and caters to personal needs. Encourage the participation of the entire work force in decisions involving individuals and communities.
Motivational Tactics	Allow people to do what they enjoy. Help workers to be creative. Provide an environment where people merge their lives with their work in positive, emotionally enriching, and empowering ways.

DISCUSSION

The Arts and Crafts movement popularized handmade furniture and furnishings while spearheading a social movement that celebrated rustic life. A powerful force in the late 19th and early 20th centuries, the movement exerted a strong and ubiquitous influence on management styles and strategies of motivation.

with joy instead of slaving in drudgery. In upstate New York, he founded the Roycrofters, a company based upon Arts and Crafts principles that produced products of high quality and did so by hand.

During its high point, the Arts and Crafts movement exerted a profound influence upon social theory that extended far beyond popular fashion and taste. Rustic life, handcraftsmanship, and their impact upon psychic wellbeing were celebrated. An overview of the Arts and Crafts movement is presented in Table 1–1.

Thus, the Arts and Crafts movement celebrated rural life and portrayed rustic people in heroic ways. William Morris in Britain, and Elbert Hubbard in the United States, emerged as major tastemakers and social reformers who advocated a return to a more simple and rural mode of existence.

As with many other social movements, the vogue of the Arts and Crafts movement has passed, but it continues to cast a long shadow; its significance and influence has never died. Today, many indigenous, ethnic, and traditional people face circumstances that are similar to those 19th century.

Parallel social theories

Advocates of the Arts and Crafts movement often merged their philosophical beliefs with partisan goals. Morris and Hubbard, for example, combined business with activism by advocating socialist ideas even while promoting their economic and social experiments within a capitalistic environment. The overall effectiveness of Morris and Hubbard appears to have been subdued because both had one foot in the practical business world while the other stood in opposition to it.

Towards the end of the 19th century, however, many of the issues addressed by the Romantics and the Arts and Crafts movement were paralleled by the emerging social theories of the era, including the work of German sociologist Ferdinand Tönnies (Cahnman 1973) and French anthropologist Emile Durkheim (Thompson 1982).

Tönnies was a member of a prosperous family that resided in a rustic German region that had been annexed by Denmark. As a result of his background, Tönnies was familiar with small, intimate communities that dominated the countryside. Tönnies' childhood experiences, furthermore, provided insights regarding the impact of economic change upon the hinterland and its people. This thinking led him to envision a distinction between different types of societies and patterns of social organization. He presents these differences with reference to what has come to be known as the Gemeinschaft vs. Gesellschaft dichotomy.

Gemeinschaft refers to small-scale, intimate communities, warm social networks, and interpersonal relationships that were solidified by strong emotional and collective bonds. Tönnies suggested that this form of social organization is typical in small-scale and traditional societies and communities that, typically, are found in the hinterland. People in Gemeinschaft communities interact on a face-to-face basis, usually in cooperative fashion typified by an egalitarian orientation.

The alternative form of social structure is the Gesellschaft which is more formal, rational, and complex. This arrangement is more prominent in urban settings that are characterized by individualism, impersonal relationships, and wage labor. Significantly, in Gesellschaft communities, the close, intimate relationships that typify Geminschaft communities break down or become weaker with self-interest (and even the exploitation of others), often emerging as an accepted norm. In other words, the comfort and the safety net provided by a Geminschaft social environment is stripped away.

Tönnies had a long and productive life and he made many contributions to social theory. A sad, but significant, badge of honor is the fact that in old age he was exiled from Germany because he was critical of Nazi policies and actions.

In France, Emile Durkheim made similar observations. He also discussed the transition from a rustic, rural existence in terms of a growing dominance of urban life. In Durkheim's case, he portrayed these differences with reference to what he called "Mechanical" vs. "Organic" social structures.

Mechanical societies are small scale and close-knit. In such rustic communities, most people know each other and regularly interact on a face-to-face basis. As a result, they tend to understand and empathize with each other. The differences between people are relatively insignificant and specialization is not pronounced. Because the community is close-knit, the amount of alienation, dysfunction, and misunderstanding that people experience tends to be reduced. As a result, many mechanical societies possess less stress and psychological pain than those who live in an organic environment (or are making a transition towards it).

10 A social background

In organic societies, in contrast, relationships are much more formal. More rigid social structures emerge. A distinct division of labor arises. Instead of possessing generic skills and knowledge, specialization becomes the norm. The differences between various social groups grow to the point where different segments of society may have trouble understanding or effectively interacting with one another.

On the other hand, this formal and highly structured character allows the society to gain efficiency through the specialization of its various parts. The various components of an organic community fit together to form an interrelated and complex entity comprised of components that have distinct functions. Durkheim notes that this pattern dominates complex, urban societies. When this occurs, different social classes, professions, institutions, belief systems, and so forth combine in ways that help the society to function more effectively and efficiently. Durkheim also observed that as this organic trend becomes increasingly evident, the social and psychological needs of some people might not be adequately addressed. Thus, the requirements needed for a complex society to function more effectively can simultaneously undercut the needs of specific individuals and/or groups.

Although specialists in social theory might recognize and focus upon differences between Tönnies and Durkheim, their work is largely parallel. These seminal social scientists independently invented similar paradigms regarding the how urban migration effects people. The theories of Tönnies and Durkheim, furthermore, parallel the perspectives of the Romantic era and the Arts and Crafts movement regarding how urbanization and psychological pressure can increase stress.

A comparison of Tönnies and Durkheim is presented in Table 1–2.

TABLE 1–2 Tönnies and Durkheim Compared

Issue	Tönnies	Durkheim
Description	Based on the degree of ruralness vs. urbanization, significant differences exist in how people relate to each other and interact.	Significant differences exist in the ways people relate to each other and interact based upon the degree of ruralness vs urbanization.
Rural	*Gemeinschaft*: Small scale. Face-to-face. Mutual understanding. Intimacy.	*Mechanical*: Small scale. Face-to-face. Mutual understanding. Intimacy.
Urban	*Gesellschaft*: Complex. Impersonal. A strong division of labor.	*Organic*: Complex. Impersonal. A strong division of labor.

DISCUSSION

Both Tönnies and Durkheim noted that urbanization and industrialization were transforming how people interact. Their parallel approaches demonstrate recurring issues of late 19th-century sociology involving shifts in society that are similar to the Romantic movement, the Arts and Crafts movement, and social commentators such as Charles Dickens.

Perhaps the models of Tönnies and Durkheim can be critiqued on the grounds that they tend to overstate their basic premises. Doing so, however, is a common, rhetorical tactic and not necessarily the result of sloppy thinking.

To their credit, both Tönnies and Durkheim appear to have independently invented a way of viewing a profound transition from rural to urban life that was taking place in Europe in the 19th century. Their work is reinforced by the humanities and the liberal arts. Although these sociological paradigms might need to be tempered, clarified, or refined, both appear to have identified and discussed a profound social trend and its implications. The fact that two seminal social theorists came to similar conclusions in this regard is revealing.

Additional orientations

So far, two trends have been discussed. One is from the liberal arts. The other is based upon social theory. Eventually, a more applied extension of these ideas emerged largely from social planners. Patrick Geddes and Lewis Mumford are examples of this movement.

In the late 19th and early 20th centuries, Patrick Geddes spoke of the three concepts of "folk, work, place" as a means of evaluating options. Geddes, you may recall, was a prominent social planner who sought to mix social change with cultural and architectural preservation in a nurturing and empowering manner.

In this regard, Geddes observes: "Planning . . . to be successful . . . must be folk planning. This means that its task is not to coerce people . . . against . . . [their] wishes. . . . Instead its task is to find the right [solutions for] people" (Geddes 1947).

Geddes believed that the structures and patterns of communities profoundly influence social relationships and the quality of life. An early example of Geddes' efforts involves Edinburgh, Scotland's "Old Town", that had long been the most depressed and dilapidated part of the city. He revitalized the area and to this day many of the buildings he restored continue to be a part of the University of Edinburgh campus. A keystone of the project was his Outlook Tower, a museum of regional and world history. Significantly, Geddes sought to nest his projects within a specific cultural milieu instead of relying upon universal social principles (as more "rational" and scientific planners were prone to do). This strategy is extremely important to those who believe that social and economic development needs to be adapted to local circumstances and not simply be based upon generic and standardized plans.

Perhaps Geddes vision is best expressed by his work in India when he was providing advice for architecture plans involving Bombay. The assignment led Geddes to write: "What town planning means under the Bombay Town Planning Act of 1915", where he advocated principles such as (1) going beyond superficial beauty in order to enhance human life and energy, (2) preserving buildings of historic and religious significance, (3) not merely imitating European cities in order to create a community that would build local pride, and (4) focusing on the wellbeing of all, instead of catering exclusively to the well-to-do.

12 A social background

Geddes consciously sought an alternative to the industrial world and he advocated creating environments that served the people. He recognized that the ways of the West should not be embraced by all.

Others, such as Lewis Mumford (Miller 1989), were also influenced by these sort of perspectives. Mumford coined the word "technics" to expand beyond technology, including both the skills and the social context triggered by technological change and its impacts. In *Technics and Civilization*, Mumford acknowledged that other societies and civilizations reached a high degree of technical skill without allowing these practical aspects of life to completely dominate. Mumford observed that these people were skilled and informed, but embraced different goals, hopes, and ambitions.

Social planners and economic development specialists working with indigenous, ethnic, and rural people can learn from Mumford when he points to the limitations of technology and warns of the changes they initiate. Emphasizing that contemporary tools and technologies should not be viewed as universals that should be sought by all, Mumford provides the rationale needed to rebut those who embrace technology and the modern world in chauvinistic ways.

Mumford also refers to what he calls "megamachines" which, in essence, are profoundly powerful ways of organizing people and resources. Thus, in *Technics and Civilization*, Mumford suggests that the key invention leading to the modern age was not the steam engine or any such device, but the clock. Once clocks were able to precisely measure time, leaders and employers could more effectively regulate the workforce in ways that were an efficiency that many lament has ceased to be humane. Before the clock, "hourly work" and tight scheduling, as we now accept them, could not exist. Thus, the clock, as a tool for controlling humanity, revolutionized economic life and encouraged people to adhere to the demands of the production floor, not their feelings or the laws of nature.

Combining these views, a pattern can be seen. In earlier times, society appears to have focused largely around human needs. As cultures became more complex and urban, the prerequisites of society, not the needs of individual people, emerged as increasingly central. Various intellectuals, activists, and organizational leaders have fought against serving organizations in ways that thwart people and undercut human feelings. Nevertheless, the trend towards catering to the needs of organizations has steadily increased; in the process, the complaint is often made that people have lost ground. This raises the question: "How will individuals and communities respond to this transition?"

The concept of anomie

Tönnies and Durkheim (and others) were concerned with the impact of society upon people. They noted a shift away from small-scale, intimate communities towards impersonal systems for controlling people and harnessing their efforts in increasingly organized and efficient ways. Anecdotal accounts regarding the pain and suffering that could result from this transition were sometimes included in such analyses. Nevertheless, a formal and systemic account of such potentials was not emphasized. This gap was filled by Durkheim's theory of anomie that addresses the pain associated with a transition from a mechanical to an organic way of life.

Durkheim presents anomie as a condition of confusion and social instability, resulting from a breakdown in the collective values, morals, expectations, yardsticks of evaluation, principles, and so forth that are held by society. Such misunderstanding and confusion could arise when a community or its people make a transition from a mechanical to an organic way of life. When these transformations are rapid and unexpected, adjusting in appropriate ways can become difficult.

Consider, for example an indigenous, ethnic, or rural community that is introduced to rapid, unexpected change that is not mitigated in a positive and constructive manner. Under such circumstances, people are likely to lack the skills needed to effectively function in the emerging environment. Even if the people operate successfully on a day-to-day basis, they might feel uncomfortable doing so. This situation can lead to alienation, unhappiness, and sorrow. Such a situation can be described as anomie.

Durkheim dealt with anomie in his study of suicide (1893) where he presented statistical evidence that different forms of suicide result from a number of distinct causes or motives. Altruistic suicide, for example, results from a desire to help others or to achieve a socially acceptable goal (such as a soldier sacrificing his life to save his comrades). In addition, Durkheim demonstrated that suicide might result from the impacts of anomie caused by the breakdown of the social standards that normally regulate behavior in ways that lessen alienation or sorrow. Thus, changing environmental conditions can result in people acting in deviant ways, including suicide, as well as other responses such as ignoring the norms of society.

Consider the situation that Charles Dickens describes in in *Oliver Twist* where the urban wasteland has become the world of young gang members. Certainly, the need for food, clothing, and shelter was a motivator. But according to the anomie-based theories of Albert Cohen, something else was probably going on (Cohen 1955, 1965). Cohen observed that the most common form of juvenile delinquency involves gang membership. He goes on to suggest that, to a large degree, individuals in gangs commit crimes to gain social status among their peer group. In a world plagued by anomie, gang members strive for success and recognition, at least among their friends, by successfully performing according to the rules of the street.

When a social system is in a state of anomie, the established norms of society cease to be adequately understood and/or accepted. New values and meanings, however, might not immediately arise. According to Durkheim, such conditions lead to a sense of sorrow, a lack of purpose, and despair. If anomie becomes intense, struggling against impossible odds can appear to be useless, causing people to give up. Dysfunctional behavior can result. Indeed, Durkheim (1893) indicates an increased suicide rate (a form of dysfunctional behavior) is correlated with anomie.

14 A social background

In other words, anomie can trigger social problems and dysfunctional behavior. This is a key issue and the foundational concept of this book. Alternatives or antidotes to anomie will also be discussed.

Economic development, even when positive and needed, can contribute to anomie. As a result, anomie might fuel hurtful side effects that need to be anticipated, addressed, and mitigated. Many examples of this possibility exist. Recall the work of Alvin Toffler, who in *Future Shock* (1970) analyzed the profound impact which social and economic changes exert upon those who live in the West and the other developed regions of the world. Arguing that unrelenting change can result in profound and tragic implications, Toffler argues that social change (wrought by snowballing technological transformations) can reap staggering emotional, cultural, and social costs if left unchecked and unmitigated.

Thus, Toffler's perspectives are consistent with the observation that changes in the industrialized West can create social and economic disruption capable of triggering an epidemic of anomie. In the less developing regions, where social change wrought by outside forces are far more pronounced, the impacts can be expected to be even more troublesome. American novelist Thomas Wolfe's *You Can't Go Home Again* (1940) portrays George Webber as a man who returns to his hometown only to find that during his absence things have profoundly changed. Alienated from a world that has been irrevocably transformed, Webber realizes his home no longer exists; as a result, he cannot go home again. Wolfe wrote a fictional example of anomie that Toffler described decades later in *Future Shock*.

Discussion

In the 19th century, rural Europeans were coming into contact with powerful outside forces. As a result, the way of life experienced by these people was disrupted, often with hurtful consequences, as dramatized by writers such as Charles Dickens.

Methods of mitigation were suggested, including the examples provided by Arts and Crafts leaders including William Morris and Elbert Hubbard. Social planners (such as Patrick Geddes and Louis Mumford) also contributed to the conversation.

In this environment, Emile Durkheim offered the concept of anomie that suggested that rapid social change can trigger tensions and sorrow capable of driving people to dysfunctional psychological responses. As will be discussed in later chapters, Durkheim was the first to articulate this profound causal relationship that decision makers seeking economic and social change need to consider.

Discussion questions

(1) The first wave of the industrial revolution took place in the West during the 18th and 19th centuries. Discuss the social changes wrought by this demographic and technological transformation. Are there parts of the world where

What is anomie? **15**

this type of adjustment is currently taking place? If so, what challenges are faced by these communities and their people?

(2) Discuss the Romantic Movement as an alternative to the Industrial Revolution and other rational systems of economic development. Compare with the tenets of the Enlightenment. How did William Morris and Elbert Hubbard call for more socially and culturally sensitive economic policies? Provide your own evaluation of their perspectives.

(3) Compare Tönnies and Durkheim. What does the similarities in their work suggest regarding the conditions in Europe in the 19th century? Do indigenous, ethnic, and traditional people in developing regions face similar circumstances? Why or why not?

(4) Envision the work of Patrick Geddes and Louis Mumford as extensions of the Romantic vision and the Arts and Crafts movement. What clues do they provide to those who are dealing with cultural enclaves facing rapid change due to economic development?

(5) The Highland Clearance that took place in Scotland in the 18th and 19th centuries is an example of forcing people to abandon their small, close-knit communities in order for the landowners to pursue new economic opportunities. Envision such actions as a trigger for anomie. Can you imagine similar anomie-causing events in today's world? If so, describe.

References

Ashton, T. S. (1948). *The Industrial Revolution (1760–1830).* (Oxford, UK: Oxford University Press).

Bate, P. H. [1901] (1972). *The English Pre-Raphaelite Painters: Their Associates and Successors.* (New York: AMS Press).

Cahnman, W. J. (ed.) (1973). *Ferdinand Tönnies: A New Evaluation.* (Leiden: Brill).

Champney, F. (1983). *Art & Glory: The Story of Elbert Hubbard.* (Kent, OH: Kent State University Press).

Cohen, A. (1955). *Delinquent Boys.* (New York: Free Press).

Cohen, A. (1965). "The Sociology of the Deviant Act: Anomie Theory and Beyond." *American Sociological Review* 30: 5–14.

Coote, S. (2018). *William Morris: His Life and Work.* (Baton Rouge, LA: Third Millennium.

Durkheim, E. (1893). *Suicide Translated by John Spaulding and George Simpson.* (New York: The Free Press, 1951).

Geddes, P. (1947). "Reports on the Towns in the Madras Presidency (1915)" In: Tyrwhitt, J. (ed.) *Patrick Geddes in London* (p. 22). (London: Humphries).

Miller, D. L. (1989). *Lewis Mumford: A Life.* (New York: Weidenfeld and Nicolson).

Morris, W. (2003). *News from Nowhere.* ed. Leopold, D. (New York: Oxford University Press).

Naylor, G. (1971). *The Arts and Crafts Movement: A Study of Its Sources, Ideals and Influence on Design Theory.* (London: Studio Vista).

Richards, E. (1982). *A History of the Highland Clearances: Agrarian Transformation and the Evictions, 1746–1886.* (London: Croom Helm).

Smith, L. C. (1968). *Consider the Lilies.* (London: Gollancz).

Thompson, K. (1982). *Emile Durkheim.* (London: Routledge).

Toffler, A. (1970). *Future Shock.* (New York: Random House).

16 A social background

Wolfe, T. (1940). *You Can't Go Home Again*. (New York: Harper Collins, 1989).

Relevant terms

Anomie   According to Emile Durkheim, the alienation and disorientation that takes place when rapid change makes life unpredictable and potentially meaningless to people.

Arts and Crafts movement   A political, social, and stylistic movement that emphasized handcraftsmanship, meaningful work, and rural life.

Bombay Town Planning Act   A document written by Patrick Geddes that advocates urban planning that take the needs of people into account and develops the environment to reflect the desires and feeling of the people.

Dickens, Charles   British writer who drew attention to the negative implications of the industrial Revolution in novels such as *Oliver Twist*.

Durkheim, Emile   French anthropologist/sociologist who was concerned with the transition from rural to urban life and its implications.

Enlightenment   A philosophic movement of the 17th/18th centuries that emphasized the benefits of rational thought and action.

"Folk, work, place"   A slogan used by Patrick Geddes to draw attention to individual, emotional, and community aspects of urban planning.

Future Shock   A book by Alvin Toffler that deals with the (often negative) impacts of change upon people.

Geddes, Patrick   British urban planner who focused upon the emotional and community implications of development.

Gemeinschaft   According to the Tönnies model, small, rural, and close-knit communities.

Gesellshaft   According to the Tönnies model, urban, industrial, and rational communities.

Highland Clearance   The eviction of rural farmers in Britain in order to use large sections of land for sheep herding.

Hubbard, Elbert   An American leader of the Arts and Crafts movement.

Industrial Revolution   An economic movement that resulted in objective, rational decisions in business, wage labor, urbanization, and so forth.

Megamachines   A term coined by Lewis Mumford to describe phenomena that profoundly influence the way people live and are controlled in modern, technologically oriented communities.

Morris, William   A British advocate of the Arts and Crafts movement.

Mumford, Lewis   A futurist, influenced by Geddes who focused upon the power of technology and ways in which it needs to be controlled.

News From Nowhere   Utopian novel by William Morris that advocated a return to the lifestyles and means of production of the Middle Ages.

Pre-Raphaelites   Tastemakers and philosophers of the mid-19th century who looked to the people of the Medieval era as role models to be emulated by the modern world.

Romanticism   A response to the rationalistic Age of Enlightenment that focused upon feelings and emotions.

Technics   A term coined by Lewis Mumford to indicate the profound impacts of technology upon life.

Toffler, Alvin   An American futurist whose work is concerned with the hurtful impact of rapid and uncontrolled change.

Tönnies, Ferdinand   Late 19th-/early 20th-century German sociologist who wrote about the transition from rural to urban life and the implications of the resulting changes.

2

COPING WITH ANOMIE

Learning objectives

Sociologist Robert Merton expands the theory of anomie by discussing various responses to the hurtful impacts of change. Some reactions are dysfunctional; others are positive. This analysis leads to a discussion of strain theory and its emphasis upon social tensions. Although anomie and strain theory typically examine deviance within homogeneous populations, they can also deal with distinct cultural groups.

Specifically, this chapter offers insights regarding:

(1) Robert Merton's adaptation and expansion of Durkheim's views of anomie.
(2) Merton's typology of different ways in which people respond to anomie.
(3) How strain theory expands anomie to deal with deviance in a homogeneous culture.
(4) Revising anomie and strain theory to deal with distinctive groups of peoples.
(5) Using anomie and related concepts to deal with social and psychological dysfunction among indigenous, ethnic, and rural peoples.

Durkheim's anomie and its limitations

As discussed in Chapter 1, anthropologist Emile Durkheim developed the concept of anomie to deal with the tensions and alienation caused by rapid and unmitigated social change and urbanization. Durkheim's pioneering investigations regarding suicide set the stage for analyzing the relationships between (1) anomie that is triggered by cultural transformations and (2) dysfunctional behavior exhibited by those who experience these changes.

Essentially, Durkheim portrays anomie as an inconsistency between (1) the standards of socially acceptable behavior and the goals embraced by a people and

18 A social background

(2) the perceived ability to achieve these goals in a socially acceptable manner. When the inconsistency between these phenomena is great, the rules of society tend to deteriorate or break down.

As is often the case with discoveries and intellectual innovations, Durkheim's pioneering work was incomplete; although he provides a specific example of anomie (as correlation with suicide rates), he did not deal with its full range of influences. It was left for later contributors to fill in gaps that Durkheim left unaddressed. That later thinker was Robert Merton, who made significant and invaluable advances to Durkheim's work. Merton, however, was primarily concerned with relatively homogeneous cultures, not cultural enclaves being transformed by powerful external groups and forces.

The contributions of Robert Merton

Starting in the late 1930s (Merton 1938) and extending thereafter, Robert Merton (1968) expanded Durkheim's concept of anomie. One of his major contributions was exploring how and why anomie occurs. Merton's basic premise is that society provides individuals with (1) goals to which they should aspire, and (2) conventional and acceptable methods for achieving these objectives.

Merton, however, understood that over time, the social structure (and/or the socio-economic milieu in which a community exists) might evolve in ways that inhibit the ability of people to attain sanctioned and honored achievements in an acceptable manner. The resulting confusion, tension, and discontent can lead to anomie. Merton also recognized (as Durkheim did before him) that under such conditions, the predisposition for deviant and/or dysfunctional behavior can increase.

Merton's lasting achievement is that he directed attention towards a variety of ways in which people might respond to anomie. By doing so, he expanded and operationalized Durkheim's work by providing a typology of reactions that can occur. Significantly, Merton realized that some of these options are more fruitful than others. To demonstrate his position, he offered a typology of five distinct responses to anomie including: (1) Conformity, (2) Innovation, (3) Ritualization, (4) Retreatism, and (5) Rebellion (Merton 1938). They can be described as:

> *Conformity* is a situation where people continue to embrace the goals of the society and seek to achieve them in the traditional, socially acceptable manner. Conformers continue to respond in the way they did before the pressures causing anomie were present. Conformity is a conservative response and it preserves traditional relationships between people. Conformity, however, can inhibit the ability to adjust to new conditions.
>
> *Innovation* is a situation where people continue to seek the goals of society while using new methods that might not be socially acceptable. Mainstream sociologists often characterize these maneuvers as illegal, antisocial, or deviant. Among indigenous, ethnic, and traditional people, however, innovation might include responses that, while violating traditional norms or expecta-

tions, can exhibit more effective results. If so, embracing productive, but taboo, strategies for achieving socially acceptable goals might ultimately contribute to cultural preservation and adaptation.

Ritualization is a situation where the person follows the norms of society but loses track of the goals to be achieved, causing them to act in a rote manner using tradition as a behavioral guideline. Unfortunately, the costs vs. the benefits of their actions are not addressed. Doing so can easily generate hurtful results. When people follow the old ways merely as an end in itself, the ability to respond in a practical and beneficial manner is reduced.

Retreatism is a situation where the person rejects both the cultural goals and the institutionalized methods for achieving them. Although people reject the status quo, they do not necessarily embrace any positive or beneficial alternative. If so, counterproductive behavior, such as alcohol abuse, is likely to increase. While under the influence of alcohol or drugs, for example, the victim might be temporarily distracted from the plight faced, but fail to respond in an effective manner.

Rebellion is a situation where the person (1) rejects both the goals that society provides and the traditional means of achieving them, while (2) simultaneously embracing substitute goals and methods. Under such circumstances, the break with the old ways is profound and complex. Chaos might result. Different factions might arise in conflict with one another. The situation created by widespread rebellion can be particularly painful to those who continue to embrace tradition and/or fear change. These variants are presented in Figure 2–1.

Institutionalised means

	Accept	Reject
Accept	Conformity	Innovation
Reject	Ritualism	Retreatism

Cultural goals

New means

New goals — Rebellion

FIGURE 2–1

20 A social background

TABLE 2–1 Responses to Anomie

Response	Description	Analysis
Conformity	The traditions of the culture are preserved. People and the community continue to be motivated and act as in the past.	The community and its culture are stable, but strategically responding to circumstances is minimal. Relatively little positive adaptation.
Innovation	Although the goals of society remain intact, people embrace new methods for achieving them.	Although maintaining the goals of the community, the means of achieving them evolves to reflect new circumstances.
Ritualization	People continue to act according to the old conventions of behavior although doing so has little ad hoc value.	Although the ways of the past continue to be embraced, strategically responding to new conditions is insignificant.
Retreatism	People withdraw from or abandon the old ways, but do not embrace a new alternative.	Psychologically, people are cut off from their heritage. Dysfunctional responses are likely.
Rebellion	New goals and new codes of behavior are embraced.	People replace both the traditional goals and the strategies that are used to achieve them.

DISCUSSION

When indigenous, ethnic, and traditional people confront change and anomie, a number of possible responses exist. The way people respond can have far-reaching consequences for the health of the people and their strategic responses, both individually and collectively.

As presented by Merton, anomie can spawn a wide variety of responses that are directly related to how individuals and the community deal with the pressures faced. These alternatives are compared in Table 2–1.

Merton's expansion of anomie, therefore, points to a wide variety of responses regarding circumstances that prevent people from achieving socially acceptable goals in socially acceptable ways. Some of these options can lead to positive and constructive responses; others tend to be counterproductive. This richer portrayal usefully expanded Durkheim's work.

Strain theory

Over time, Merton (and others) expanded this broader model of anomie in order to deal with deviance and crime that occurs in mainstream society. These refinements have emerged as *strain theory*, a sub-discipline of sociology and criminology (Agnew 1992; Agnew 1997; Featherstone and Deflem 2003).

This manner of dealing with atypical behavior was useful to Merton because he embraced a structural approach that tended to assume that all people (or a vast majority) within a culture share very similar beliefs, morals, attitudes, ways of acting, and so forth. As a result of this assumed social homogeneity in thought and action, strict structural models deemphasize social tensions/strains within society as well as significant individual variations. Behavior that does not reflect the norm is deemphasized. Merton needed an explanation for deviance because it contradicted the structural paradigm that was the foundation of his work.

In reality, of course, many people act in divergent ways, leading Merton to seek a method that could account for crime and deviant behavior within the context of structural social theory. Merton's enhanced depiction of anomie did so by describing people caught with no clear choice of action by being unable to achieve socially acceptable goals in a socially acceptable way. When this situation occurs, tensions and strains develop as people find it is impossible to live according to their ideals.

People who act in an "innovative" manner, for example, might embrace the goals provided by society (such as a need to be "successful"), even though these socially acceptable objectives might be accomplished in an unsanctioned or unacceptable manner (such as shady or illegal behavior). Another option is "ritualization", in which people accept underachievement or failure in order to act and live in a culturally appropriate manner. Individuals following both of these paths simultaneously respond to their culture and its dictates in some ways while ignoring other social conventions and expectations.

Many people find themselves in situations where they must choose between (1) achieving acceptable goals or (2) conducting themselves in an acceptable manner. These people are at a risk to develop some sort of psychological dysfunction because of strains and pressures stemming from their culture and heritage. They, however, simultaneously maintain a connection with their traditions and seek the comfort and guidance it potentially provides.

On other occasions, people (1) reject both the goals and methods provided by their heritage while adopting no alternatives (retreatism) or (2) they embrace new goals and methods (rebellion). In these cases, people discard important components of their heritage and risk losing an important bulwark against suffering.

Social and psychological dysfunction is especially likely when neither the methods nor the goals provide a comfortable emotional foundation. In the case of retreatism, both goals and methods are rejected, but no alternative replaces them. Lacking an established social and moral compass, people can find themselves marooned in a confusing and meaningless world. Under these conditions, alcohol and/or drug abuse is likely to arise (beginning, perhaps, as a temporary relief from such confusion and alienation).

Those exhibiting a pattern of rebellion, in contrast, embrace new goals and methods after rejecting their traditions. Such people can easily find themselves psychologically vulnerable if new and untested way of thinking and/or acting are unfulfilling or fail to provide adequate comfort.

The results of these responses are likely to be dysfunction. As Durkheim observed in the 19th century, dysfunctional responses (even suicide) can emerge

22 A social background

as an attractive option when people are caught in the grip of anomie caused by cultural changes and strains.

Thus, Merton's revision of anomie and strain theory provides a robust and useful model regarding deviance and psychological dysfunction. His version is tailored to relatively large and homogenous communities in which most people embrace the same heritage and traditions. Under some conditions, however, various traditions and tenets of that structure break down. When this happens, people can find themselves on a weak psychological footing that increases the likelihood of dysfunctional responses.

After Merton envisioned his versions of anomie and strain theory, others have sought to fine-tune his work. Robert Durbin (1959), for example, expands Merton's criteria from five to 14. Although Durbin's work is more precise and detailed, it also emerges, in my opinion, as unwieldy and overly complicated. In addition, Durbin felt that Merton's focus upon socially sanctioned goals and socially acceptable methods for achieving them was inadequate and went on to emphasize the influence of individual goals, experiences, education, and so forth. Doing so appears to reflect challenges and critiques that structural analysis was facing when Durbin wrote. Popular poststructural and existential models, for example, center upon the thinking of individual people, not the uniform responses of collective groups. Durbin appears to be responding to this trend. Although poststructural models are very useful in many contexts, the analysis in this book centers upon competing social structures, the potential tensions between them, and how this pressure can trigger dysfunction. Other revisions and expansions of anomie and strain theory exist, but space prevents a full discussion.

Thus, although Durkheim's views of anomie are concerned with the plight of distinctive social groups (such as Gemeinschaft communities as discussed by Tönnies), strain theory is designed to deal with homogeneous populations, the stress and tensions within them, and the responses of those impacted.

In order to use these models to deal with specific cultural enclaves, a return to Durkheim's emphasis upon distinctive groups is useful. By doing so, particular groups, such as indigenous, ethnic, and traditional people and their responses, can be more easily and appropriately analyzed.

From macro to cultural distinctiveness

Because indigenous people, ethnic groups, and traditional enclaves tend to be distinct from the larger population, the prevailing conceptions of anomie and strain theory often need to be adjusted to deal with groups facing significant and, perhaps, unmitigated change.

The following adaptation, while embracing many of Merton's advances, envisions a distinctive pattern in which (1) cultures are in conflict, (2) choices and adaptations arise, (3) the resulting conflict causes strain, (4) which leads to pain

Coping with anomie 23

and uncertainty, with (5) the resulting pain and uncertainty triggering dysfunction. Each step in this process will be briefly discussed.

Cultures in conflict: When social and/or economic development takes place, distinctive communities are often strongly encouraged (or forced) to adjust in ways that reflect or mesh with the opportunities and/or demands that arise. Doing so potentially conflicts with the mores and traditions of the people.

Choices and adaptations arise: When economic development projects are initiated (often due to promptings from intrusive outsiders), choices and adjustments must be made. In many cases, doing so is at odds with the local culture and its traditions.

Conflict causes strain: These choices can cause conflict within the community because the new options might conflict with the heritage and established protocols of the community. These conflicts can cause stress and strain within the community.

Strain causes pain and uncertainty: The resulting stress and uncertainty can lead to an increase in the pain and uncertainty faced by the community or some segment of it.

Pain and uncertainty lead to dysfunction: Significant pain and uncertainty, especially if unmitigated, can lead to psychological dysfunction.

This process is portrayed in Table 2–2.

TABLE 2–2 Anomie and Strain Faced by Distinctive Cultural Enclaves

	Analysis
Cultures in conflict	During periods of significant change, outsiders often introduce or mandate new methods, priorities, and so forth, which might conflict with local traditions.
Choices/ adaptations	The local community and its members must make decisions regarding what adaptations will be made and what traditions will be maintained.
Conflicts cause strain	These choices can be painful. Decisions might emerge as compromises resulting in lost opportunities and/treasured traditions becoming vulnerable and passé.
Strain causes pain	The resulting confusion and loss can cause emotional pain, suffering, and alienation.
Pain causes dysfunction	These hurtful situations can trigger psychological dysfunction.

DISCUSSION

Anomie can contribute to psychological dysfunction. As a result, activities such as economic or social development that bring significant change and stress need to be recognized as a source of potential dysfunction.

24 A social background

Thus, the discussion of anomie needs to expand beyond analyzing the structure of homogeneous communities; by doing so, distinctive cultural enclaves and people who find themselves caught between two worlds can be better served.

Dealing with cultural differences

As discussed, the theory of anomie was originally developed as a method for dealing with cultural differences and the alienation and stress that can result from conflicts between different ways of life. Thus, Durkheim was concerned with (1) the process of moving from a mechanical (traditional) to an organic (modern, industrial) culture, (2) the pressures this transition puts upon people, and (3) the psychological dysfunction that could result from cultural and economic transitions.

Robert Merton was more concerned with relatively homogeneous cultures and why people within such standardized communities choose to disregard some mores, laws, and codes of behavior. Merton tended to depict a disregard for established norms such as crime or deviance. His work gave rise to strain theory that is commonly used to explore why people act in ways that conflict with their cultural norms.

This book, in contrast to Merton's emphasis, deals with cultures and communities that are divergent from the prevailing social structure and/or its dominant influences. These distinctive peoples are often asked to adhere to mainstream codes of behavior or action even when doing so conflicts with the norms of the local community or the culture of origin. This is very different from Merton's orientation.

Nevertheless, Merton provides a crucial advance by focusing upon a wide array of possible responses to anomie and cultural strain. This typology is useful even if those being examined are not members of the mainstream culture. In such cases, people are asked to abandon or disregard their cultural traditions or heritage in order to embrace another competing system that might be exerting significant economic, social, or political leverage.

This is the manner in which anomie will be examined in this book.

Discussion questions

(1) What was the major advance that Robert Merton provided to the theory of anomie? Does his work make applications of the theory more useful and pragmatic? Why did Merton focus upon a relatively homogenous society and deal with alternative behavior accordingly? How can this perspective be useful?
(2) Discuss how strain theory is an expansion of the concept of anomie. Discuss how it deals with deviance and criminal activities within a relatively homogeneous culture. What blind spots can emerge from such a perspective?
(3) Why is dealing with distinctive ethnic groups difficult using Merton's focus upon cultural homogeneity? Was Emile Durkheim also concerned with cul-

tural homogeneity? Can the theory of anomie be revised to deal with cultural variation? Is this useful when dealing with indigenous, ethnic, and traditional people? Why or why not?

(4) Discuss specific ways to use anomie and related concepts when dealing with social and psychological dysfunction among indigenous, ethnic, and rural people. Are these applications distinct from working with homogenous populations? Why or why not?

(5) Discussing an indigenous, ethnic, or traditional group of your choice, compare a homogeneous structural approach similar to Merton's, with an account that can more effectively deal with local distinctiveness. Which method do you think is more appropriate? Why?

References

Agnew, R. (1992). "Foundation for a General Strain Theory." *Criminology* 30 (1): 47–87.

Agnew, R. (1997). "The Nature and Determinants of Strain: Another Look at Durkheim and Merton." In: Agnew, R. & Passas, N. (eds.), *The Future of Anomie Theory* (pp. 27–51). (Boston, MA: Northeastern University Press).

Durbin, R. (1959). "Deviant Behavior and Social Structure: Continuities in Social Theory." *American Sociological Review* 24: 147–163.

Featherstone, R. & Deflem, M. (2003). "Anomie and Strain: Context and Consequences of Merton's Two Theories." *Sociological Inquiry* 73 (4): 471–489.

Merton, R. K. (1938). "Social Structure and Anomie." *American Sociological Review* 3 (5): 672–682.

Merton, R. K. (1968). *Social Theory and Social Structure*. (New York: Free Press).

Relevant terms

Anomie   Confusion, bewilderment, alienation, and so forth caused by changes in society which undercut the norms of society.

Conformity   A response to anomie in which people continue to act in conventional ways.

Durkheim, Emile   French anthropologist/sociologist who developed a pioneering theory of anomie.

Innovation   A response to anomie in which people embrace new means of achieving socially acceptable goals.

Merton, Robert   An American sociologist who explored a variety of ways in which people can respond to anomie.

Rebellion   A response to anomie in which people replace both the goals of society and the socially acceptable means of achieving them.

Retreatism   A response to anomie in which people reject both the goals of society and the means of achieving them, but do not replace them.

Ritualization   A response to anomie in which people adhere to traditions for their own sake and with the knowledge that doing so will not be practical or effective.

Strain theory   Using the theory of anomie to deal with deviance and crime. Can be adapted to deal with any group that changes its behavior and orientations due to anomie.

3
HURTFUL IMPACTS OF ANOMIE

Learning objectives

Anomie often impacts people who are subjected to social and economic development projects that cause significant change. Specific examples are analyzed with reference to possible hurtful impacts. The relevance to economic development, business, and social work is analyzed. In particular, the following issues will be addressed:

(1) The relevance of Frantz Fanon as a trained mental health professional, in spite of violent and radical tendencies.
(2) The novels of Chinua Achebe as a classic description of hurtful anomie leading to dysfunction.
(3) The Ghost Dance of the 19th-century American Indians as a community-wide embrace of a dysfunctional fantasy leading to counterproductive decisions and increased sorrow.
(4) The Cargo Cult as a delusion that encouraged people to embrace unrealistic hopes in ways that wasted their efforts in hurtful and counterproductive ways.
(5) The causes and implications of dysfunctional responses to anomie and social strain.

Introduction

The first two chapters dealt with how the theory of anomie can model significant responses to social and economic change. Contemporary uses of the theory of anomie, however, tend to focus upon mainstream cultures, not distinctive groups of people such as indigenous, ethnic, and traditional peoples. Nevertheless, perspectives regarding anomie and social strain can be adapted for examining divergent populations. Emile Durkheim's seminal discussions of anomie were overtly designed to do so.

In this chapter and the next, the theories of anomie and strain theory are discussed with reference to particular cultural enclaves. Chapter 3 discusses dysfunctional examples. Chapter 4, in contrast, focuses upon more fruitful and productive reactions.

The theory of pain and dysfunction

Economic and social development are often agents of disruptive change. Their influences and side effects can cause pain, social turmoil, and psychological dysfunction. On some (but not all) occasions, colonialism and neo-colonialism exerts a role in this regard. A large number of writers, thinkers, and activists have dealt with this reality. Frantz Fanon, an Afro-American of Caribbean origin, who was a trained mental health professional, provides an excellent example of such thinkers.

Even though he was a partisan who championed hostile views, the work of Frantz Fanon provides a useful introduction to the pain that can be caused by change. Born and raised in the French colony of Martinique, Fanon had all of the advantages of middle-class life. A black man from the American Caribbean, Fanon was brought up to believe his race and colonial origins were insignificant (Bandy 1979, 250) and that he was, above all, a Frenchman. Fighting with the Free French during World War II, however, Fanon quickly learned differently. The equality and respect that he anticipated did not exist for him. The anger resulting from his second-class treatment led Fanon to produce an array of strongly written manifestos urging colonial and post-colonial peoples to throw off their Western influences and allegiances.

In *Black Skin, White Masks* (1952), for example, Fanon lamented that indigenous people often use yardsticks deriving from Europe as measures of their own worth and achievements. Emerging as an advocate of bloodshed, violence, and revolution in *The Wretched of The Earth* (1965), Fanon's aggressive diatribes are sprinkled with insights regarding the impact of Westernization upon a population unprepared for its onslaught. In general, Fanon advises: "Let us decide not to imitate Europe; let us combine our muscles and our brains in a new direction" (Fanon 1965, 253).

Although Fanon was a revolutionary who advocated violence, he stands apart from the mere propagandist or rabble rouser. The depth of his vision stems from Fanon's training and experience as a clinical psychiatrist who had seen firsthand how being caught between two worlds can be a catalyst for anguish and mental illness. One of the insights of *Black Skin, White Masks* is that colonialism, post-colonialism, and neo-colonialism can create hurtful stereotypes causing indigenous people to be written off as inferior and second class. Fanon observes that under such circumstances many people "seek to escape through assimilation – by adopting a 'white mask'" (Wakeman 1972, 458).

Starting his career as a psychiatrist who treated patients after they developed the symptoms of mental illness, Fanon eventually offered preventive

28 A social background

medicine: developing strategies to eliminate the tensions, traumas, and inconsistencies faced by indigenous people in a changing world. Fanon states his goal is to "prevent man from feeling a stranger in his own environment". In the final analysis, this "could not be achieved by treating the man. It was the environment that must be changed" (Wakeman 1972, 458).

Fanon's achievement was to document potentially negative side effects of assimilation and cultural homogenization, which are thrust upon people who are ill-prepared or unwilling to abandon their traditional ways. Although I disagree with Fanon's contention that violence is inevitable and should be encouraged, he does point to a host of hurtful maladies, which potentially result from the unmitigated impacts and economic intrusions.

Fanon's life is as revealing as his writings. He was a global sophisticate who circulated among the great European intellectuals as an equal. He was a trained mental health professional who ultimately turned his back on Europe and the West. Fanon's life, as well as his writing, dramatizes the emotions of people caught between two worlds and the negative potentials that can be caused by the resulting tension.

What Fanon experienced is clearly consistent with the models of anomie and strain theory advanced by Durkheim, Merton, and others. This is especially true in situations where these perspectives are broadened to deal with cultural enclaves, not merely alienated members of homogeneous cultures. Key to Fanon's work is the observation that significant dysfunction can occur when the cultural heritage and identity of a people are profoundly weakened in an unmitigated manner.

Fanon, therefore, presents a particularly hostile and aggressive discussion of the pressures of anomie and cultural stress. In order to deal with the implications of these perspectives, examples from the colonial/post-colonial literature of Nigeria will reinforce these concepts.

Expanding the theoretical background

Those who wish to understand the full consequences of Westernization can profit from the novels of Third World authors who reflect upon the impact of the colonial era. The celebrated trilogy of Chinua Achebe, the prominent Nigerian author, for example, provides especially profound insights regarding the pain associated with unwanted Westernization, personal disenfranchisement, cultural breakdown, and social disruption.

Those hoping to understand the full impact of anomie and cultural strain can profit from Achebe's *Things Fall Apart* (1958), which deals with the first inroads of the British into Nigeria in the 19th century. Achebe begins with a nostalgic and idyllic picture of life before the colonial era. He depicts friends playing games, people following the routines of everyday life, the give and take of intimate family conversations, and so forth. Although not all these vignettes directly relate to the plot, they document a good life that existed in an earlier era.

The main character, Oknokwo, is a symbol of the past who represents those who are so connected to their tradition that they cannot adapt. Sentenced to a seven-year exile by the village elders, Oknokwo's absence coincides with the coming of Christian missionaries, the undermining of the traditional culture, and the growing political power of the colonial officials. Returning from exile, Oknokwo is unable to cope with the termination of his way of life and, after murdering a colonial official, he commits suicide in the appropriate, traditional way. In short, Oknokwo's reactions and behaviors provide a textbook response to unmitigated anomie.

Achebe, furthermore, provides other examples of hurtful responses to anomie including attempts to achieve acceptable goals in unacceptable ways. In *No Longer at Ease*, the third installment of his trilogy, Achebe continues his analysis of outside intervention and social dysfunction by portraying Obi Oknokwo, grandson and namesake of the ill-fated hero of *Things Fall Apart*. Instead of representing illiterate vestiges who are unable to adapt, Obi was trained at a Western university, speaks perfect English, and dresses in the Western style. He longs to transform his government to fit the Western mold. Obi is the true cosmopolitan: a prime example of the Westernization of indigenous people.

Surprisingly, the novel begins with Obi on trial for accepting bribes. The judge comments that he cannot understand how someone with such great opportunities and potential could have stooped so low and for no apparent reason. The rest of *No Longer at Ease* (1969) dissects Obi's life to show how the tensions of being caught between two cultures inevitably lead to his downfall.

Together, these two accounts portray a panorama of people who respond to anomie in hurtful ways. In *No Longer at Ease*, furthermore, we see that anomie and alienation can arise among those who appear to have made a productive transition to the modern world.

These characterizations by Achebe closely reflect the models of anomie presented by Durkheim, Merton, and strain theory that describe what happens when the rules and norms of society break down after the transformations caused by economic, technological, and cultural change.

Anomie typically creates discomfort because people no longer know how to act and/or understand what to expect from others. As the heritage and traditions of earlier times fade or are weakened, shared norms, beliefs, hopes, and expectations are unable to unite people in a positive, compelling, and constructive way. When this happens, hurtful and dysfunctional responses can easily result.

As discussed earlier, Robert Merton argues that a key cause of anomie is the disparity between the goals that society gives to people, coupled with an inability to achieve them in a socially acceptable manner. When this unhealthy situation arises, anomie is the likely result (Merton 1957, 121–194). To be specific, Merton argues that the mores and norms of a society provide its members with goals to which they should aspire, on the one hand, and socially acceptable methods of achieving these objectives, on the other. Over time, however, the culture (or the socio-economic milieu in which it exists) might change to such a degree that its members can no longer achieve sanctioned and honored goals in socially

30 A social background

acceptable ways. When this happens, the stress confronting people tends to escalate, often with horrific results.

Merton went on to suggest that when people cannot achieve their goals in socially acceptable ways, the propensity for deviant and counterproductive behavior increases. The events described by Achebe clearly reflect this potential.

Having dealt with relevant fictional accounts of anomie and culture strain and the hurtful reactions they can spawn, two real-life examples are discussed: the Ghost Dance and the Cargo Cult. Like Achebe's novels, they portray how a changing world can result in poor choices by the community and psychological dysfunction among individuals.

The Ghost Dance

People confronted with the pain and stress caused by outside contact often respond in bizarre ways. Two such examples are the Ghost Dance (Mooney 1896; Kehoe 1989) and the Cargo Cult (Harris 1974; Inglis 1957; Worsley 1957).

The Ghost Dance was an influential religious movement among Native Americans during the late 19th century. Its most prominent leader was a visionary named Wovoka who intertwined aspects of local traditions with a new religion. Some of Wovoka's recommendations involved living in a moral, harmonious, and more productive manner. These suggestions are positive and productive aspects of the movement.

Others predictions and recommendations, however, were counterproductive and hurtful. Wovoka, for example, taught that if a certain dance was properly performed, the dead ancestors would come back to life, herds of buffalo would return, the white intruders would go away, and the old way of life would be restored. None of these projections, unfortunately, reflected reality. Acting according to them proved to be a tragically counterproductive strategy.

Some devotees were even convinced that if they wore "ghost shirts" they could not be killed by the guns of the white man and, therefore, victory was assured. Followers, furthermore, believed that Wovoka could perform miracles, such as healing the sick. The emerging Ghost Dance movement and religion appealed to many indigenous people who had suffered grievously due to reservation life, sickness, cultural decline, and governmental policies that sought to undercut their heritage. Sadly, Ghost Dance activities led to the massacre at Wounded Knee, the last major bloodbath of the wars between the United States and the American Indians.

Viewed from the perspective of anomie, the Ghost Dance can be viewed as an example of conformity in which the traditions of the culture were largely preserved and embraced, albeit in an unproductive manner. People were encouraged to look to the past, ignore reality, and act in counterproductive ways that sometimes blurred into suicide. By doing so, the actual circumstances faced were not addressed in any meaningful manner and caused the situation to deteriorate even further.

The Cargo Cult

The Cargo Cults of Melanesia involve indigenous people whose lives were hurtfully transformed and disrupted by unprecedented outside contact. In the early 20th century, white intruders appeared, bringing social and economic changes with them that led to chaos among the local people. The disenfranchised indigenous population attempted to reassert control over their lives by pathetically copying the very activities that were tearing their world apart.

The specific responses to these hurtful circumstances are well known. When intrusive foreigners began to gain a foothold in Melanesia, members of the indigenous community noticed that these powerful outsiders built airports and harbors and then waited for airplanes and ships to arrive with great wealth. Apparently, the local people, becoming desperate and jealous, wanted their share of the cargo. One ploy they used was to build phony airports in the misguided belief that by doing so they could magically attract their own supernatural airplanes and gain affluence as a result.

Although such responses are typically associated with some charismatic leader, a common explanation is that these Cargo Cults are responses to sorrow, fear, and anxiety caused by rapid and uncontrolled change. The Cargo Cults (although associated with ignorance and superstition) appear to have arisen out of desperation, hopelessness, and disappointment.

Viewed from the perspective of anomie, the Cargo Cults can be described as innovative and/or rebellious responses to the failure of traditional methods. Devotees of the cult, for example, embraced new ways to achieve goals (luring cargo-carrying planes by building bogus airports) even though other aspects of the society appear to have remained intact.

This behavior might also be reflective of rebellion in which new goals (a desire for Western goods brought by planes) was accompanied by new economic strategies (building airports to attract planes). In any event, a major adjustment (although counterproductive) took place that responded to profound tensions in the culture and economy that had been caused by rapid and unmitigated outside contact.

The reason for introducing these examples is to emphasize that a strong potential exists for people to make counterproductive decisions when they face hurtful and unprecedented disruptions that undercut their culture, heritage, and traditional way of life. The theories of anomie and strain theory can be used to model these changes. With this in mind, the Ghost Dance and the Cargo Cult are compared in Table 3–1.

People facing change often have trouble understanding the situations they face. When this happens, they can become confused and desperate. Effective responses can become difficult. The Ghost Dance and the Cargo Cult are two extreme examples of people caught up in dysfunctional responses to unmitigated change. Under these conditions, a significant segment of the population began to act in psychologically dysfunctional ways. The results were tragic and counterproductive.

32 A social background

TABLE 3–1 The Ghost Dance and Cargo Cult Compared

Issue	Ghost dance	Cargo cult
Trigger	Cultural stress. Economic reversals.	Cultural stress. Economic reversals.
Response	A belief in personal invincibility, coupled with the supposed magical return of ancestors and the old way of life.	A misguided and ill-informed copying of the techniques used by outsiders that had threatened the traditional way of life.
Impact	Suicidal behavior. Reliance upon magic.	Counterproductive economic strategies.

DISCUSSION

The Ghost Dance and the Cargo Cult represent hurtful and unproductive responses to change, stress, and anxiety that can be modeled by the theories of anomie and strain theory. If cultures are to successfully cope with change, they need to avoid dysfunctional alternatives such as these.

Behavior of this type needs to be curtailed and replaced with more appropriate and functional alternatives.

More productive alternatives

As acknowledged, these two examples document extreme and blatantly pathological responses to change. They draw attention to less overt reactions that, although dysfunctional and counterproductive, might go unrecognized. Thus, on many occasions, the responses of people could appear to merely be unsophisticated reactions to new circumstances. Although limited experience is often a contributing factor, some form of anomie and/or reactions to it are also likely to be present. Addressing these factors and mitigating their negative potential is profoundly important.

Although the Ghost Dance and Cargo Cults point to damaging and ineffective reactions, the action of other local communities demonstrate that some indigenous, ethnic, and traditional peoples have charted a more productive path. A key message of this book is that although people are thrust into the modern world and forced to experience profound changes, dysfunction and cultural destruction is not inevitable.

It is possible, in contrast, for cultures to respond in positive and constructive ways that maintain their unique character and distinctiveness even if significant adjustments to destabilizing conditions must occur. If so, positive and beneficial cultural revitalization may result.

The responses of the Iroquois Indians of New York State (USA)/Ontario (Canada) and the Yup'ik of Alaska (USA) are good examples. They will be evaluated in the next chapter.

Discussion questions

(1) Discuss the importance of Frantz Fanon as a commentator regarding the impact of the colonial/post-colonial era.
(2) Discuss Fanon's work with reference to the mental health of indigenous, ethnic, and traditional peoples. Fanon was trained as a mental health professional. How do you think this fact influenced his views? What other factors might have contributed to his views?
(3) The novels of Chinua Achebe depict how the colonial influence and its legacy can trigger psychological dysfunction. Does Achebe depict this as a short phase that is quickly overcome? If not, how should social and economic intrusions into hinterland communities be mitigated? Discuss from the perspective of anomie.
(4) The Ghost Dance of the 19th-century American Indians involved a broad, community-wide embrace of a dysfunctional fantasy that led to counter-productive decisions and hurtful dysfunction. The Ghost Dance was popular among people who did not have modern education and lacked the insights of science. Can we attribute their flawed thinking merely to this fact? What other factors might have contributed to the popularity of the ghost dance?
(5) The Cargo Cult involved a delusion that led to irrational hopes and wasted efforts in the quest for prosperity. Discuss from the perspective of anomie. How can efforts such as these work against the best interests of people?
(6) List and describe five hurtful and dysfunctional responses of anomie and social strain with reference to indigenous and traditional communities.

References

Achebe, C. (1969). *No Longer at Ease*. (London: Heinemann).
Achebe, C. (1958). *Things Fall Apart*. (London: Heinemann, 1989).
Bandy, F. (1979). "Frantz Fanon: Black Orphans of the Homeless Left." *Encounter*, pp. 25–29.
Fanon, F. (1952). *Black Skin, White Masks* (Translation of *Peau Noire, Masques Blancs*, 1952). (London: MacGibbon & Keen, 1967).
Fanon, F. (1965). *The Wretched of the Earth* (Translation of, 1961). (New York: Grove Press).
Harris, M. (1974). *Cows Pigs Wars and Witches: The Riddles of Culture*. (New York: Random house).
Inglis, J. (1957). "Cargo Cults: The Problem of Explanation." *Oceania* 27 (4).
Kehoe, A. B. (1989). "Death or Renewal?" *The Ghost Dance: Ethnohistory and Revitalization* (pp. 32–33). (Washington, DC: Thompson Publishing).
Merton, R. (1957). *Social Theory and Social Structure*. (Glencoe: Free Press).
Mooney, J. (1896). *The Ghost Dance Religion and Wounded Knee*. (New York: Dover Publications).
Wakeman, J. (1972). *World Authors: 1950–1970*. (New York: Wilson).
Worsley, P. (1957). *The Trumpet Shall Sound: A Study of Cargo Cults in Melanesia*. (London: MacGibbon & Kee, 1957).

Relevant terms

Achebe, Chiuna Influential Nigerian novelist who explored the hurtful implications, demands, and legacies of the colonial era.

34 A social background

Black Skin, White Masks Book by Frantz Fanon that suggests that indigenous, ethnic, and traditional people suffer because they evaluate themselves with reference to the criteria of the developed world.

Cargo Cult An attempt by indigenous people to gain prosperity by superficially copying the techniques of the West in a quest for economic wellbeing that had proved to be futile and counterproductive.

Fanon, Frantz Author and activist who urged indigenous people to acknowledge who they are and live accordingly.

Ghost Dance An American Indian movement and uprising that was a response to rapid and uncontrolled change. A counterproductive phenomenon, it created additional sorrow and maladaptation.

No Longer at Ease Novel by Chinua Achebe that suggests that even indigenous people who appear to have successfully assimilated themselves into a Western lifestyle can be hurt by the loss of their heritage or their alienation from it.

Things Fall Apart Novel by Chinua Achebe that deals with cultural icons being displaced by changes brought by the colonial era.

Wretched of the Earth Book by Frantz Fanon that emphasizes that Third World people will be wretched until they learn to follow their own path.

4

POSITIVE RESPONSES TO ANOMIE

Learning objectives

Although anomie often has negative and dysfunctional influences, people, communities, and cultures sometimes respond to it in a positive and constructive manner. This potential is portrayed in the novels of James Fenimore Cooper and Chinua Achebe. The real-life successes of the Iroquois Indians and the Yup'ik of Alaska present historic instances of progress and success. In specific, this chapter will:

(1) Consider how the novels of James Fenimore Cooper explore the anomie and displacement caused by outside forces taking control in a hinterland. Cooper provides clues regarding how self-awareness can help people avoid dysfunction.
(2) Analyze how Chinua Achebe portrays an indigenous leader who adapts in order to cope with the pressures of outside intervention by a powerful colonial empire.
(3) Introduce Handsome Lake, a Native American leader who, although similar in some ways to Wovoka of the disastrous Ghost Dance movement, offered productive strategies for overcoming anomie and for rebounding from despair and defeat.
(4) Examine the Yup'ik, a Native Alaskan people hurtfully impacted by change. Their history reflects both the work of Emile Durkheim regarding dysfunction and suicide and Handsome Lake's vision of cultural renewal.
(5) Synthesize the implications of these examples via a general discussion regarding positive reactions to change and anomie.

Introduction

Chapter 3 discussed situations where responses to anomie were hurtful and dysfunctional. Examples, including the Ghost Dance and the Cargo Cult, demonstrated

36 A social background

that when unmitigated change comes too quickly (and possesses traumatic ramifications), people often fail to respond in a positive and productive manner. Just the opposite: their actions are apt to be counterproductive and hurtful.

These examples, and others that parallel them, serve as a warning for communities caught in a pattern of rapid and unmitigated social and/or economic development. They also provide warnings to outsiders who encourage change and, perhaps, are agents of or catalysts for it.

The possibility of pain, strife, and dysfunction, however, should not blind us to the fact that on some occasions people respond in a healthy and fruitful manner. Hopefully, more people can be prompted to avoid destructive and dysfunctional reactions, while strengthening their communities and the people within them. If so, psychological dysfunction can be reduced as positive adaptations are encouraged and supported.

James Fenimore Cooper and positive adaptations

Responses to anomie that are productive and positive can help people mitigate the disorienting pressures of change that exist in their lives. As was the case in Chapter 3, the discussion of this possibility begins with a review of insightful fictional accounts before graduating to historic examples.

The classic frontier novels of James Fennimore Cooper portray those shoved aside by the onslaught of civilization as well as the disruption and trauma caused by the intrusion of "civilized" settlers into the hinterland of North America. (For more details, see the chapter on James Fenimore Cooper in Walle 2000.) Besides creating immortal literary figures, Cooper points to healthy strategies that rural and ethnic enclaves can embrace in order to adjust to the threats, transformations, and disruptions brought by outside invaders.

Introduced in *The Pioneers* (1823), Cooper's classic character, Natty Bumppo, is an old frontier scout who long served white settlers struggling to establish farms and towns on the frontier. Even though Bumppo battles the indigenous people of the region, he is more akin to his indigenous opponents than to the immigrants he serves.

After aiding these invaders for many years, Bumppo finally succeeds in driving out his indigenous rivals; as a result, Western civilization comes to dominate the region. At this point, the old scout and his way of life come in conflict with the emerging norms of the encroaching newcomers he long served. It is now Bumppo's turn to face the hurtful and confining pressures of civilization.

Specifically, the wise old frontiersman, following his way of life, hunts as he always has in order to satisfy his legitimate needs. Doing so, however, violates ill-conceived hunting regulations set up by the new, civilized regime; as a result, Bumppo runs afoul of the law. In the end, the man who tamed the frontier is cast out by the community that could never have been established without his frontier prowess.

Cooper, however, does not allow his character to wallow in an abyss of sorrow, loss, and dysfunction. Bumppo abandons society and civilization, returning to a world where he can live on his terms and creates a place for himself. He is last seen disappearing into the yet untamed forest with his long rifle and trusted dog.

Bumppo returns in a sequel, *The Prairie* (1827), in which the Great Plains are depicted as a world where civilization cannot compete or establish itself. In this environment, the old hunter and his indigenous cohorts are able to carry on in a manner of their own choosing. Cooper places the action in what he calls "The Great American Desert", a region depicted as unsuited for complex urban life. Because civilization cannot follow, this region provides a haven for less complex ways of life, such as those practiced by Bumppo and his indigenous friends. Bumppo is able to endure these challenges without serious trauma or psychological dysfunction because the old frontiersman never forgets who he is; he possesses an emotional grounding that provides the strength needed to prevent dysfunction in the face of change and adversity.

Due to modern science and technology, of course, it has become increasingly possible for urban and technological societies to exist and exert an influence wherever it wants. As a result, Cooper's depiction of an ecological barrier to civilization is no longer as valid as it once was (although global warming might change that). And yet, Bumppo's inner strength reveals that non-mainstream people can avoid the ravages of a hurtful anomie by remaining aware of who they are, recognizing what is important to them, and acting accordingly.

Expressed in terms that Durkheim would have understood, Bumppo comes from a rural and close-knit "mechanical" background. Although he long served a more highly structured "organic" community, Bumppo is aware of his distinctiveness and does not embrace the alien way of life. Because of this self-awareness and personal resolve, Bumppo remains strong, well-adjusted, and able to avoid dysfunction even when facing hardship.

Achebe's vision of fruitful adaptation

One way to extend Cooper's vision is to return to the work of Chinua Achebe who, as we saw in the last chapter, presents the examples of Oknokwo and Obi Oknokwo who (consistent with the theory of anomie) emerge either as suicidal or antisocial due to the profound social changes that they endure. Achebe portrays these characters as drifting into dysfunction due to the decline of their indigenous culture, the pressures of the colonial and post-colonial eras, and the profound void created by cultural strain. Achebe's vision, however, is not totally pessimistic as demonstrated by *Arrow of God* (another novel in his trilogy), where he introduces Ezeulu, who acts in a positive and productive manner that reinforces and protects his culture and its heritage.

Unlike the saga of James Fenimore Cooper, Achebe's trilogy does not provide a convenient haven to which his character can retreat. The colonial regime established by Great Britain is pervasive and cannot be avoided. After the events in *Things Fall Apart* (1958), *Arrow of God* (1964) takes place a few years after Oknokwo commits suicide; the novel tells the story of Ezeulu, a local chief who strategically struggles to protect his village and maintain its way of life by adapting to colonial

38 A social background

rule, not by overtly confronting forces that cannot be defeated. Even though he chooses the path of accommodation, Ezeulu does not abandon his heritage and traditions. When Ezeulu's son embraces Christianity (many Ibo became Christian during the colonial era), for example, the wily old chief sends the boy to a mission school so he can spy on the whites. Thus, profound change (presented as religious conversion) simultaneously works to help preserve the heritage, traditions, and ways of life of the people. The new ways of Christianity and the old culture, it seems, become intertwined, mutually influencing and stabilizing one another. Change does not completely supplant or destroy tradition.

Ezeulu represents responses to anomie that are functional and positive. His example demonstrates that even when profound change is taking place some people are able to adjust to it in positive and constructive ways. Cooper and Achebe, therefore, both point to constructive adjustments that can take place under hard and hurtful circumstances. Even though they wrote about different continents and are separated by over a century, their messages parallel each other.

In Achebe's work, as with Cooper's, a mechanical way of life coming to grips with an emerging organic environment is portrayed. Although adjustments must be made, the local culture and their people are not pathetic, hopeless, and inevitably destined to oblivion.

Having presented fictional accounts, we will now turn to real-life examples.

From fiction to history

The foregoing examples are fictional and based intuitively upon perceived trends, not facts. Nevertheless, the authors provide useful insights regarding change, the maladies that are often associated with it, and how to cope.

Having drawn upon imaginary examples in order to develop useful perspectives regarding change, social transformations, and economic development, historical examples will demonstrate how actual people responded. One example concerns the Iroquois Indians of the early 19th century. Coming from the same region where James Fenimore Cooper's Natty Bumppo originated, the Iroquois experienced horrific pain and suffering due to unrelenting change, but they were able to regroup in positive and productive ways. A second example concerns the Yup'ik of Alaska, a Native group that suffered grievously even when their "quality of life" seemed to be improving when evaluated with reference to the "social indicators" typically used by economic development specialists and consultants.

Significantly, although separated by time and place, these two examples parallel each other in revealing ways. Each is discussed separately before the relevance of their similarities is discussed.

The renaissance of the Iroquois

The Iroquois of New York State (USA) and the Province of Ontario (Canada) are noteworthy as an indigenous people who have been able to preserve their

Positive responses to anomie **39**

heritage even while adapting to new conditions. (For more details see Walle 2004.) Politically astute, in the 18th century, the Iroquois were able to stand on an equal footing with the colonial forces of Britain and France. In the first half of the 18th century, they gained wealth and power by doing so.

During the French and Indian War, known as the Seven Years War in Europe (1754–1763), the Iroquois fought alongside the British and were rewarded accordingly. After the French were defeated, however, the British took total control of North America and found themselves without other European rivals. With the French defeated, the British had little need for indigenous allies. Under these conditions, the Iroquois were "no longer able to play off the British and French against each other and [they found themselves] surrounded by a circle of British forts" (Wallace 1969, 442). As might be expected, when the British saw no strategic need in catering to the Iroquois, the generosity long lavished upon them faded. Economic support dwindled; suffering crept in.

This was the situation until the North American colonists rebelled against Britain in the Revolutionary War (1776–1783). Once again, the Iroquois became embroiled in a conflict that was larger than their world. Realizing that the British valued the region merely for trading purposes while victorious colonial settlers would probably be tempted to migrate into Iroquois territory, most Iroquois sided with Britain. Their decision was rational and well-reasoned, but it proved to be costly:

> [During the war, the Iroquois homeland] was devastated by the John Sullivan [United States military commander] expedition in 1778, which in a three pronged offensive managed to burn the houses and the crops in almost every major Iroquois town. Many of the women and children, and the surviving warriors, took refuge at Fort Niagara with the British, who housed them in a refugee camp, inadequately clothed, inadequately fed, inadequately sheltered, and swept by disease. By the end of the war, despite their military successes, the Iroquois population had been cut approximately in half.
>
> *(Wallace 1969, 443)*

After the war, the victorious United States, remembering that the Iroquois had been their enemy, showed them few favors. And, as the Iroquois had feared, White pioneers were attracted to the area. By the turn of the 19th century the Iroquois were beaten in war, decimated by diseases brought by the Whites, stripped of much of their land, and besieged by new economic rivals. The results of this unenviable situation included infighting, personal resignation, despair, and retreat. As is often the case under such circumstances, dysfunctional behavior (including alcoholism) became rampant.

Anthropologist Anthony Wallace, an Iroquois specialist, points to the widespread dysfunction that arose among the Iroquois, including violence, uncontrolled weeping and pining, fear of peers (as evidenced by accusations of witchcraft),

40 A social background

social disunity, and widespread alcoholism. Clinical depression was commonplace and Wallace observes that when people were sober, they were likely to be suicidal (1969, 196–201). With the culture and its people in total disarray, the Iroquois, as a viable culture, were headed towards extinction.

Within this milieu of cultural decline, Handsome Lake, a once respected indigenous leader, had fallen into hopeless alcoholism and his productive life appeared to be over. By the spring of 1799 he was "bedridden, reputedly . . . as a consequence of prolonged [alcoholism]" (Wallace 1969, 445).

In June of that year "Handsome Lake collapsed [and] appeared to have died, but actually he was in a trance state and was experiencing the first of a series of visions in which messengers of the Creator instructed him in his own and his people's religious obligations" (Wallace 1969, 445). After recuperating, Handsome Lake dedicated his life to sobriety and to the restoration of Iroquois culture and society.

On the one hand, Handsome Lake encouraged his people to embrace their cultural traditions in innovative ways. The late 18th and early 19th century had devastated the Iroquois, throwing their culture in a state of complete disarray. Economically, the Iroquois could not effectively compete with the new settlers who entered the region. Although embracing and championing Iroquois culture, Handsome Lake also recognized that Iroquois society needed to adjust to the emerging economic realities in order to rise again.

Iroquois men, for example, focused upon hunting and warfare and viewed farming as an unmanly and shameful profession that was left to women. When white settlers migrated into Iroquois territory, however, new methods of farming (that included men performing their share of the work) proved to be more efficient and productive. The success of these outsiders further undercut the Iroquois economy. Under these circumstances, Handsome Lake encouraged Iroquois men to take up farming and he urged them to perceive agriculture as a legitimate profession, not a source of shame or embarrassment. This change of attitude helped the Iroquois to rebound economically.

This response, suggested by Handsome Lake, is clearly an example of what Robert Merton describes as an innovative response to anomie in which the goals of society remain intact although people are provided with new methods for achieving them. Although Merton's view of anomie often associates innovation with harmful and hurtful substitutes such as illegal activities, in the case of the Iroquois, innovation involved a productive and legitimate rethinking of traditional sex roles. It allowed the Iroquois to adjust in positive ways to emerging social and economic circumstances.

Handsome Lake, furthermore, forcefully denounced the disruptive and dysfunctional responses exhibited by his people. Drinking alcoholic beverages, in particular, was banned, along with promiscuous sexual behavior, the practice of witchcraft, and other troublesome habits that were undercutting the society and its people. Handsome Lake went on to insist that people acknowledge their past errors and refrain from similar misdeeds in the future.

From the perspective of anomie, Handsome Lake seems to have intuitively understood that many people had fallen into responses that resemble retreatism; they had abandoned the old ways but had not replaced them with any positive alternative. Demanding that people find a meaningful focus, he began to combat social and individual degeneration.

Largely through Handsome Lake's example and message, the Iroquois people reversed their downward spiral of decline and re-emerged as a vital and viable culture. To this day, they continue as a powerful force. This example emphasizes that ethnic and rural groups beset by disruptive change can adapt to changing circumstances by tempering and transforming their traditions in productive and strategic ways. Cultures are powerful forces and they often provide invaluable tools for both physical survival and for psychological health. In addition, cultures are capable of innovation and change.

The Yup'ik of Alaska

Approximately 175 years after Handsome Lake's achievements, Alaska Native Harold Napoleon provided another example of cultural renewal. Napoleon's *Yuuyaraq: The Way of Being Human* (1996) examines his indigenous people (the Yup'ik of southwestern Alaska), focusing upon the trauma and stress caused by contact with the outside world during the 20th century. Napoleon chronicles the plight of a beaten and bewildered people who fell into disarray and dysfunction before beginning the process of healing and renewal.

Instead of being a scholar or professional researcher, Napoleon is an insightful layman who recovered from a personal bout with alcoholism. Writing at a subjective and intuitive level, Napoleon discusses the horrible and traumatic events that undercut Yup'ik society (as well as the positive steps that can be taken to insure its renewal). Revealingly, these observations and recommendations independently duplicate the example and suggestions of Handsome Lake.

While not excusing or discounting his lapses and personal responsibilities, Napoleon points to the destructive power of uncontrolled social and economic change as well as the alienation and disruption they can produce. Although communities and individuals might have fallen into a pattern of dysfunction, he insists these hurtful responses can be overcome through strengthening and revitalizing the local culture and its heritage.

Napoleon points to the irony that profound decline among the Yup'ik is correlated and associated with economic progress and physical wellbeing. He notes that the people had warm clothes, comfortable homes, and enough to eat. Famines were a thing of the past. Viewed from a material perspective, life was good. Nonetheless, the suffering was profound, alcoholism was rampant, and the suicide rate rose to epidemic proportions.

Napoleon explains these responses as the fruit of cultural destruction. He recalls that in the early 20th century disease had killed many of the elders who carried the traditions of Yup'ik culture. As a result, the survivors were denied their heritage

42 A social background

and floundered emotionally as a result. Economically, moreover, the traditional subsistence lifestyle was largely rendered passé. This situation, of course, is similar to what Handsome Lake's Iroquois faced in the late 18th and early 19th centuries. The response, furthermore, was almost identical: dysfunctional behavior, mass suicide, despair, and passive resignation.

This situation parallels the events observed by Emile Durkheim in late 19th-century France. Durkheim notes that when profound and unprecedented change took place, anomie led to depression, sorrow, and confusion. Durkheim also emphasizes that under such circumstances the suicide rate significantly increased. Among the Yup'ik, the situation is parallel, including a dramatic increase in suicide.

Napoleon uses the theory of post-traumatic stress disorder (PTSD) as a metaphor to portray the painful process of stress, alienation, and dysfunction that long plagued his culture and people. PTSD, of course, is a condition in which people develop dysfunctional patterns of response as a result of being exposed to danger, fear, stress, and so forth. Speaking with reference to this disorder, Napoleon argues that rapidly changing social and economic conditions caused unmitigated stress that, in turn, triggered dysfunctional responses and behaviors that almost destroyed the Yup'ik. This ongoing process proved to be a vicious circle because as the culture became weaker, it was less able to help people cope, leading to even more profound problems.

Discussed in terms of anomie, a pattern of retreatism emerged in which people abandoned their old ways, but did not replace them with new and powerful alternatives.

A key strength in Napoleon's account is that he is not a professional social scientist or psychologist. Indeed, his status as an insightful layman who is a member of an impacted indigenous community gives his work added credibility.

A synthesis

The positive responses of the Iroquois and the Yup'ik to anomie, depression, and dysfunction are largely identical. In both cases, (1) cultural renewal combined with (2) an embrace of the local heritage and traditions (3) led to viable and effective strategies. The implication of these examples is that by nurturing and rebuilding their cultures, heritage, and traditions, people overcome their pain and find a more productive and healthy future.

A synthesis of these two examples is useful because it verifies and reinforces the findings of researches such as by Emile Durkheim and Robert Merton. The culture, heritage, and traditions of a people can be a source of strength and comfort. Rapid change, however, can undercut the ability of the culture to provide support to its people. When cultures are weakened, hurtful stress and psychological discomfort often arise (Salzman 2001; Walle 2004). Care needs to be taken to minimize this kind of negative and hurtful response. On a positive note, by being aware of cultural roots, the pain and dysfunction of anomie can be reduced and mitigated. These insights may prove useful to strategic planners, therapists, and social workers. Each will be briefly discussed.

Strategic planners: Those who develop basic strategies and tactics of economic and social development need to take into account the full implications of what they propose. Developing initiatives that are positive and empowering to the local community should be a primary goal. Not only is doing so ethically correct, it is also practical. As a result, plans should be made with an eye towards helping people choose solutions that minimize anomie and dysfunction and do so from a long-term perspective.

Therapists: The majority of psychiatrists and psychological therapists receive their training within the mainstream world. As a result, these highly trained and certified professionals may have minimal experience dealing with atypical populations that face profound social change and hurtful pressures from outside, intrusive forces. By being aware of both positive and negative responses to change and anomie, these professionals can more effectively pursue their work.

Social workers: In order to more effectively help people deal with the problems and tensions in their lives, social workers need to gain a better understanding of what is and what is not effective. When dealing with people in need, social workers are often responsible for forging effective tactics. By (1) being aware of how distinctive people tend to respond and (2) envisioning dysfunction within a context of stress, bewilderment, and confusion, helping people return to an appropriate way of life can be more readily accomplished.

Thus, strategic planners, therapists, and social workers need to remember that alternatives to anomie are essential and achievable. The positive achievements of the Iroquois and the Yup'ik are proof of that.

Discussion questions

(1) Anomie does not always lead to dysfunction. James Fenimore Cooper's work indicates that if people can maintain a vision of who they are and what is important to them, they may be able to avoid its negative impacts. From your knowledge or experience, can you provide examples of people who had the self-awareness to avoid or mitigate psychological problems due to rapid change? If so, discuss. If not, discuss modes of thinking that might lead to useful coping strategies.

(2) Just because cultures or regions are being overwhelmed by intrusive outside forces does not necessarily mean that people cannot choose effective strategies tailored to what they need and who they are. In Chinua Achebe's *Arrow of God*, we see effective responses to the forces of change and cultural stress. To what extent do you feel cultures are resilient in this manner? To what extent do you doubt such tactics are typically effective? Why or why not?

44 A social background

(3) The Iroquois leader, Handsome Lake, is superficially similar to Wokova, who was the prophet of the disastrous Ghost Dance. Wovoka's efforts led to tragic results, however, while Handsome Lake was able to help his people respond from anomie and dysfunction in a positive and constructive way. How do you explain these differences? What lessons can we learn by comparing these two examples?

(4) The Yup'ik, a Native Alaskan people, faced many of the same pressures as the Iroquois that Handsome Lake helped. And both people were able to stabilize their cultures in a positive manner. Discuss with reference to Emile Durkheim's views of anomie and dysfunction. Why is it significant that these two examples parallel each other in many important respects?

(5) Compare examples of hurtful responses to anomie with positive alternatives. What suggestions do you have that might insure a smooth transition from change to cultural and emotional stability?

References

Achebe, C. (1958). *Things Fall Apart.* (London: Heinemann).
Achebe, C. (1964). *Arrow of God.* (London: Heinemann).
Cooper, J. F. (1823). *The Pioneers.* (New York: Charles Wiley).
Cooper, J. F. (1827). *The Prairie.* (Philadelphia: Carey, Lea, and Carey).
Napoleon, H. (1996). *The Way of Being Human.* (Fairbanks, AK: Alaska Native Knowledge Network).
Salzman, M. (2001). "Cultural Trauma and Recovery: Perspectives from Terror Management Theory." *Trauma, Violence and Abuse* 2 (2): 172–191.
Wallace, A. (1969). *The Death and Rebirth of the Seneca.* (New York: Random House, 1978).
Walle, Alf H. (2000). *The Cowboy Hero and Its Audience: Popular Culture as Market Derived Art.* (Bowling Green, OH: Popular Press; Madison, WI: University of Wisconsin Press).
Walle, Alf H. (2004). *The Path of Handsome Lake: A Model of Recovery for Native People.* (Charlotte, NC: Information Age Publishers).

Relevant terms

Arrow of God A novel by Chinua Achebe that portrays indigenous people adapting to circumstances and developing techniques that preserve their culture and way of life.
Cooper, James Fenimore American novelist who explored how civilization displaces and alienates distinctive people, including indigenous populations.
French and Indian War A conflict in North America between the French and English in which the Iroquois Indians tended to side with the English.
Great American Desert James Fenimore Cooper believed the Plains were a Great American Desert where indigenous people could maintain their lifestyle. Technology, however, has eliminated this region as a haven for small-scale cultures.
Handsome Lake An Iroquois leader who helped his people rebound by both preserving the culture and adapting it to changing times.
Napoleon, Harold A Yup'ik leader who documented the impact of rapid and uncontrolled change upon the Yup'ik (and, by extension, other indigenous peoples).

The Nature of Being Human   A book by Harold Napoleon that deals with the hurtful impact of outside intervention upon the Yup'ik (an indigenous people).

Seven Years War   See French and Indian War.

Wallace, Anthony   An expert on the Iroquois who wrote about Handsome Lake.

Yup'ik   A Native Alaskan culture that was impacted by social change and epidemics of disease brought by outside contact during the 20th century.

5

EFFECTED COMMUNITIES

Learning objectives

To effectively deal with anomie, strain, and dysfunction, it is important to evaluate the people involved. First, can these cultural groups be defined as Native, indigenous, and/or traditional? Second, are these people living what can be called "mainstream", "Third World", or "Fourth World" lives? Evaluations based on multiple criteria can provide useful insights regarding the pressures facing people and their vulnerability to psychological dysfunction. Issues to be addressed include:

(1) Connecting anomie (and dysfunction likely to stem from it) to specific types of communities.
(2) Discussing the terms "indigenous", "Native", and "traditional" and their relevance.
(3) Drawing a distinction between Third World and Fourth World as well as how these environments are likely to impact ethnic minorities.
(4) Providing a synthesis of these characteristics with an eye towards understanding the strengths and vulnerabilities of specific peoples.
(5) Analyzing these implications from a policy and strategy perspective.

Introduction

Economic development and social change occur among diverse people who possess a wide variety of characteristics. How individuals and communities respond (and the dysfunction they experience) depends, to a large degree, upon their characteristics. By understanding specific populations, better projections can be made regarding the stresses faced and the likelihood they will develop significant dysfunction.

In this chapter, social groups and the specific people that comprise them are evaluated using two different dimensions: (1) their status as "mainstream" indigenous, Native, and/or traditional people and (2) if they reside in a Third World, Fourth World, or another setting. This multi-faceted analysis provides a better understanding of people and how they are likely to react to the challenges and stresses they encounter.

Population characteristics

A key characteristic of Emile Durkheim's original conceptualization of anomie is that a variety of cultures exist. These differences contribute to their ability (or inability) to effectively deal with change. As discussed in Chapter 1, Emile Durkheim compared intimate and rural communities (that he called "mechanical") with urban and impersonal lifestyles dubbed "organic". He found that when "mechanical" people are forced to live a more "organic" existence, psychological dysfunction tends to increase. This chapter embraces and expands Durkheim's vision by dealing with a number of categories including (1) mainstream, (2) Native, (3) indigenous, and (4) traditional. By doing so, people and their communities can be discussed in a more precise manner than if only the mechanical vs. organic dichotomy was used. Each of these additional categories is discussed.

Mainstream: At an intuitive level, the mainstream population can be envisioned as the majority of people who exist in the developed world. They tend to practice a lifestyle that is reflective of what Durkheim characterizes as "organic". Wage labor, urban (or semi-urban life), and a high degree of specialization are norms. Relationships between people and groups tend to be impersonal. Although these people may possess an ethnic identity, they tend to be largely influenced and molded by urban and economic conditions, in addition to their heritage and traditions.

Native: The term "Native" (with a capital N) typically refers to people who are descended from the historic (or pre-contact) peoples associated with a region. The term is often used to identify those whose ancestors lived in an area immediately before the era of Western expansion. American Indians, the Maori of New Zealand, and Native Hawaiians are representative examples of Native people. The term "native" (with a small n) refers to someone who was born and/or raised in an area, but descended from later immigrants. According to this typology, a person of English ancestral roots born in the United States would be a "native" while an American Indian would be a "Native".

Indigenous: The term "indigenous", in contrast, typically refers to Native people who have faced (or continue to face) some sort of mistreatment or discrimination as a result of their racial, ethnic, and/or cultural identity. Consider the following definition provided by Siegfried Wiessner (1999, 60):

> indigenous people are best described as groups traditionally regarded, and self-defined, as descendants of the original inhabitants of the lands. . . . These people are and desire to be culturally, socially and/or economically distinct

48 A social background

from the dominant groups in society, at whose hands they have suffered, in past or present, a pervasive pattern of subjugation, marginalization, dispossession, exclusion, and dispossession.

According to this formal definition, not all "Native" people are "indigenous". The people of Iceland, for example, certainly fit the criteria of a "Native" people because they are descended from the first human inhabitants of the region. Native Icelanders, however, control their government and they are not persecuted or treated as second-class citizens by the regime in power. They do not face discrimination due to their racial or ethnic identity. Thus, Icelanders do not fit the criteria of "indigenous" (as described in the definition above) even though they are indisputably Native.

Traditional: Besides the terms "Native" and "indigenous", "traditional people" is another category that needs to be considered. Traditional people may or may not be descended from the original population of a region. And, perhaps, traditional people do not face discrimination. But these people possess and practice a culture that gives them a distinctiveness that is recognized both by themselves and by outsiders. A classic example of non-Native traditional people is Appalachian hill folk of the Southeastern United States. Being descendants of Scotch-Irish immigrants, they are not Native. Although there may be some slight prejudice against these Appalachians (the derogatory terms "hillbilly", "poor White trash", and "redneck" are sometimes applied to them in hurtful ways by outsiders), they are not systematically discriminated against in a pervasive manner. Nevertheless, many traditional people (such as Appalachian hill folk) share a range of concerns and pressures that are faced by Native and indigenous people. Their members, for example, often complain that their culture is being overwhelmed by the modern world and by the intrusions of outsiders.

According to the typology provided by Durkheim, traditional people tend to pursue a mechanical lifestyle that is small scale, intimate, rural, and possessing minimal specialization. This type of culture often provides psychological comfort and security. If this heritage and the relationships it fosters are undercut, psychological dysfunction is a likely result.

Some Native and indigenous people may simultaneously fit the definition of "traditional people" if they practice a lifestyle that is traditional and distinct from the mainstream population. Other indigenous and Native people may be more "modern" in their attitudes and habits. Thus, the term "traditional people" refers to lifestyle, "Native people" refers to descendants of original populations that maintain a distinctiveness that can be identified, while "indigenous people" is a term that is reserved for Native people who face (or have historically faced) discrimination, hardship, and so on because of their racial and/or ethnic identity.

A broadened view of indigenous

Today many people find the prevailing definitions of indigenous to be inadequate and they are working to expand them. Such developments are worrisome to countries that fear an erosion of their power that could occur if indigenous rights become easier to establish.

On September 13, 2007, the United Nations "Declaration on Rights of Indigenous Peoples" was passed by a vote of 111 in favor and 4 (the United States, Canada, Australia, and New Zealand) against (United Nations General Assembly 2007). Since then, these four dissenters have, in some way, embraced the declaration (even though it is not legally binding).

Key elements of the Declaration include (The Charter of Human Responsibilities 2007):

(1) Indigenous peoples have the right to self-determinism and to determine their political status.
(2) The right to distinct political, legal, economic, social, and cultural institutions, while retaining the right to participate in the life of the state.
(3) The right to establish educational systems and provide education in their own languages.
(4) The right to practice and teach spiritual traditions, to protect privacy of cultural sites and control ceremonial objects, and rights to repatriation of human remains.
(5) Indigenous peoples shall not be forcibly removed from their lands or territories.
(6) The right to development and to determine priorities for their lands, territories, or other resources.
(7) The right to determine the responsibilities of individuals to their communities.

While this declaration is not legally binding, it does point to an emerging awareness of the distinctiveness of indigenous people and a growing concern regarding their rights.

The United States voiced concern with and initially voted against the Declaration because a clear meaning of the term "indigenous" had not been agreed upon. The situation of the former residents of the Chagos Archipelago demonstrates the emerging uncertainty and confusion that can exist if clear definitions do not exist.

In the 1960s, the British depopulated the Chagos Islands in order to lease it to the United States for the construction of a military installation. The refugees took legal action opposing this action and they ultimately won their case in court. In essence, the Chagos Islanders have successfully depicted themselves as an indigenous people and the courts have acknowledged that they possess certain rights due to this fact. Thus, a document presented to the Parliament of the United Kingdom by Minority Rights Group International (2008) observed:

> Based on its 40 years of working with indigenous communities worldwide, MRG is of the view that the Chagossians do indeed constitute an indigenous people. The UK's duty towards the Chagossians must therefore be upheld in line with the rights of indigenous peoples' rights under international law.

50 A social background

The case is important because the Chagos Islanders are descended from plantation workers imported to the islands by the French in the 18th century. Thus, this people have been viewed as indigenous even though their residence on the land does not predate the era of Western expansion and, just the opposite, is an artifact of Western colonialism.

Since World War II, the term "indigenous" has almost universally referred to cultures and peoples who have a connection with their homeland that predates the modern era of political, economic, and demographic disruptions caused by the colonial era. As Janet (2002, 121) has emphasized, the contemporary view of "indigenous" arose as a practical matter that was designed to deal with issues that existed after World War II when the United Nations was formed. Specifically, the impacts of Western colonialism were major a concern during that era. In recent years, however, gaps have arisen in that arbitrary definition. Perhaps the time has come to rethink or expand what is meant by indigenous, its implications, and significance. All of this is a nightmare for governmental officials who, understandably, fear that although they may not have done nothing wrong or out of the ordinary, large chunks of their nation's sovereignty are potentially up for grabs.

Important distinctions

These terms are important because certain obstacles and vulnerabilities (as well as rights, privileges, and opportunities) may be associated with an indigenous status. In addition, the rights of Native and traditional people also need to be considered. Do people, for example, reside in Third World or Fourth World environments?

Increasingly, Native, indigenous, and traditional peoples have begun to carve out a collective identity for themselves that transcends their cultural differences. Part of this macro-identity is based upon the Third World or Fourth World environments where people live. We are all familiar with the concept of the "First World" as the capitalistic West and the "Second World" as the Eastern communist eastern bloc of the Cold War era. In those days, the term Third World was used to depict various unaligned nations that both the East and West wanted to bring under their sphere of influence.

Many of these Third World countries, that largely consist of former African and Asian countries that had formerly been a part of European colonial empires, gained their independence after World War II.

Today, with the Cold War concluded (although some envision rumblings of a revival), the definition of Third World has been transformed. The term now typically refers to countries and regions once colonized and controlled by European powers where Western immigrants never became a significant percentage of the population. As a result, upon gaining their independence, the Native populations of these countries have typically reasserted positions of power and decision-making authority, even if neo-colonial tendencies somewhat temper their de facto authority. This occurs even when internal rivalries between ethnic groups flare up to create hardship, oppression, and even genocide.

Nonetheless, the governments of these Third World countries are controlled (at least officially) by Native people. In spite of the political reshuffling that has taken place, however, the colonial era often leaves a psychological mark upon the local population. As a result, many Third World people continued to judge themselves with reference to the minority of white colonialists who were long in control and the post-colonialists who replaced them. This tendency, of course, was a major complaint of Frantz Fanon (who was discussed earlier in this book).

Since World War II, Third World intellectuals have exerted a strong influence. The work, thought, and example of Gandhi, for example, called for the people of India to affirm their identity and gain their independence. In the late 1940s, India was successful in doing so. [India, of course, is seldom viewed as a Third World country and understandably so. In addition, India is ethnically diverse. The definition of Third World used here, however, focuses upon an outside minority, British colonials in this case, having great power, but not dominating demographically. That definition reflects the situation of India during the colonial era.]

As the years went by, various African countries gained their political independence. As discussed earlier, an early and angry call for Africans to throw off the colonial mentality is Frantz Fanon's *Black Skins, White Masks* (1958), which denounces the tendency for Native people to embrace the lifestyles, priorities, and preferences of colonial role models. Fanon observed that even if indigenous people choose to wear White masks, they still have Black skins. Instead of merely embracing the beliefs and lifestyles of alien intruders and judging themselves by those alien standards, Fanon urges Native and indigenous people to accept themselves for who they are and to act accordingly. Post-colonial intellectuals, such as Fanon, have exerted a profound impact. Besides providing leadership to Third World countries, post-colonial writers have influenced intellectual movements such as existentialism, poststructuralism, and postmodernism. Post-colonial thought, in turn, has provided paradigms to academic and activist movements including Marxist analysis, feminist studies, ethnic studies programs, and so forth.

Although Fanon dealt with how indigenous people might contribute to their own oppression, other Native intellectuals, such as Chinua Achebe, explore how colonial regimes undercut and destroyed the people's heritage and traditions triggering psychological dysfunction in the process.

Post-colonial thinking (much of it coming from Africa) has exerted a profound impact by dealing with Third World situations where people, although dominated by others, remain in a demographic majority and, therefore, have the potential to re-emerge as the ruling force within their countries.

Although such situations exist in a large part of the world, they do not reflect the circumstances experienced by many Native, indigenous, and traditional people. This is because post-colonial intellectuals from the Third World deal almost exclusively with regions where the European colonial forces never became a significant percentage of the population. These perpetual outsiders functioned somewhat like "absentee landlords" who gained profits while living elsewhere.

52 A social background

In other parts of the world, in contrast, large numbers of immigrants moved into a region and made it their home. When this occurred, the Native and indigenous peoples eventually emerged as a small percentage of the population. Although Native and indigenous people still remain in these regions, they have typically become a disenfranchised ethnic group that faces hardships and discrimination due to their minority status. The term Fourth World is used here to identify such environments.

Marie Battiste and James Youngblood have called them "the unofficially colonized peoples of the world, the tragic victims of modernization and progress" (2000, 2). Representative regions where significant Fourth World populations exist include North America, Hawaii, Australia, and New Zealand.

Currently, Fourth World intellectuals are at the cutting edge of thought regarding the relationships of Natives, indigenous people, and other ethnic minorities with the larger, outside world.

Decades ago, Third World leaders such as Frantz Fanon and Chinua Achebe wrote during an angry era when the old colonial empires were being dismantled and replaced with freestanding nations dominated by Native people. Today, Fourth World intellectuals are supplementing (if not replacing) Third World intellectual leaders and offering sophisticated strategies that are aimed at helping people more effectively control their destiny. Today, the typical goal of Fourth World people is not to gain nationhood, but to achieve equity and parity within the national (and global) context in which they reside. Philosophic musings are being replaced by pragmatic maneuvers.

Talking to the leaders and intellectuals of indigenous, Native, and traditional people, the issue of "decolonialization" often comes up. In general, this term refers to a process of overcoming a wide range of influences that have often been forced upon people (or, perhaps, combines with the assimilation process as people adjust to powerful influences in their lives). In many ways, this process is similar to the course of action recommended by Frantz Fanon, who advocates people judging themselves on their own terms, not using alien yardsticks of evaluation. In any event, small, rural communities have often suffered by rejecting their heritage or because it was denied them. The process of decolonialization is offered as a means of restoring the rightful role of the local culture, heritage, and traditions.

Two illustrative examples of this emerging movement are Linda Tuhiwai Smith's *Decolonizing Methodologies* (1999, 2012) and Marie Battiste and James Henderson's *Protecting Indigenous Knowledge and Heritage: A Global Challenge* (2000). Although these books deal with specific areas (New Zealand and Canada respectively), the thinking of both expand beyond local concerns. Although the rhetoric of both books sometimes becomes impassioned, the authors seek thoughtful and reasoned solutions, not counterproductive and emotional reactions. These two representative texts (many others exist) point to a new and more reasoned path that is increasingly being taken by Native, indigenous, and traditional people. This trend is applauded.

Discussion

A basic theme of this book is that social and economic development are likely to stimulate significant change that can lead to community and individual dysfunction. This process has been explored using the theory of anomie as first established by Emile Durkheim and later expanded by Robert Merton (and those influenced by him).

In general, the theory of anomie argues that fluctuating social and economic conditions can be disruptive, alienating, and the cause of disorientation among people who are not prepared to cope with the resulting transformations. When these inabilities are pronounced, psychological pain and dysfunction are common responses.

The specific ways in which people respond, however, need to be envisioned with reference to two variables: (1) the people being analyzed, and (2) the circumstances faced. This is true because not all people are the same, circumstances vary, and these realties need to be recognized. A first step is to identify these differences using methods such as the typology of "mainstream", "indigenous", "Native", and/or "traditional" people. Having established the characteristics of specific people, the environment in which they exist needs to be considered. This can be done with reference to categories such as Third World and Fourth World. By envisioning people and their circumstances in this robust manner, effectively analyzing their specific traits becomes easier and more systematic. Presented in tabular form, these variables are analyzed in Table 5–1.

TABLE 5–1 Causes of Anomie and Dysfunction

	Third world	*Fourth world*
Native	Pre-contact people continue to dominate demographically, but lose power, status, and opportunity.	Pre-contact people who were once in the majority have been reduced to minority status due to immigration from the outside.
Indigenous	Powerful forces prevent the Native majority from equitable participation in social and economic affairs.	Attempts, overt or covert, are made to assimilate people and/or disrupt their culture and heritage.
Traditional	People who live a traditional way of life might not be allowed full participation in significant social and economic activities.	The traditional ways of life are in danger of being stripped from local cultures when distinct minorities possessing little demographic clout are subjected to forced assimilation.

DISCUSSION

Both (1) distinctive peoples and (2) a variety of circumstances exist. When evaluating the possible implications of change and anomie, both of these variables need to be addressed.

54 A social background

Preventing psychological dysfunction should be given high priority. Understanding, preventing, and mitigating anomie is a key to reducing this painful and destructive force.

The goal is to minimize, prevent, and/or mitigate dysfunction. Hopefully, by being aware of these categories and their implications, more appropriate and effective strategies can be developed.

Discussion questions

(1) A basic theme of this book is that anomie and psychological dysfunction are more likely to occur among some groups more than others. What are some of the indicators that these hurtful potentials might arise? Discuss with reference to a real or imagined example.

(2) The terms "indigenous", "Native", and "traditional" have legal and/or social significance. How can they be useful when dealing with the pressures faced by communities? The thinking regarding indigenous appears to be evolving. Who are the potential winners and losers as the term is (or is not) redefined? Why is this relevant to discussions of anomie and psychological dysfunction?

(3) Draw a distinction between Third World and Fourth World. How are these environments likely to impact ethnic minorities? These two terms seem to analyze very different situations. Explain. How might both trigger psychological dysfunction?

(4) Chapter 5 offers a discussion regarding how issues (1) involving specific types of people, (2) distinctive environment, and (3) how dealing with them simultaneously can create a more robust paradigm regarding anomie and psychological dysfunction. What are the benefits of such an approach? Is it workable? Why or why not?

(5) From a policy perspective, discuss the implications of (1) distinct people in (2) a specific environment. Focus upon social and psychological dysfunction.

References

Battiste, M. & Henderson, J. (2000). *Protecting Indigenous Knowledge and Heritage: A Global Challenge*. (Saskatoon: Purich Publications).

Fanon, F. (1958). *Black Skins, White Masks*. (New York: Grove Press; published in French in 1952).

Janet, S. (2002). *Development, Minorities and Indigenous Peoples: A Case Study and Evaluation of Good Practice*. (London: Minority Rights Group International).

Minority Rights Group International (2008). "Submission from the Minority Rights Group International." Select Committee on *Foreign Affairs Written Evidence*. Retrieved March 24, 2010 from C:\Documents and Settings\Owner\MyDocuments\ed 660\galenfall0x9\garifunalandclaims\HouseofCommons-ForeignAffairs-WrittenEvidence.mht.

Smith, L. T. (1999). *Decolonizing Methodologies*. (London: Zed Books).

Smith, L. T. (2012). *Decolonizing Methodologies* (2nd ed.). (London: Zed Books).

United Nations General Assembly (2007). *The Charter of Human Responsibilities*.

Wiessner, S. (1999). "Rights and Status of Indigenous Peoples: A Global and Comparative and International Legal Analysis." *Harvard Human Rights Journal* 12 (Spring): 60.

Relevant terms

Chagos Islanders An ethnic group that has been labeled "indigenous" even though the connection with their territory does not predate the modern colonial era.

Fourth World Regions where due to the immigration of outsiders, indigenous people have become a minority in their own homeland.

Indigenous people Native peoples who suffer (or historically suffered) as a result of their race and/or ethnicity.

Mainstream people The dominant group, often powerful outsiders, in regions where indigenous people, other ethnic groups, and so forth also live.

Native people With a capital "N", people, typically indigenous, who have long resided in a region.

native people With a small "n", people descended from outsiders who were born in a particular place and define themselves as "native".

Third World Regions where descendants of the original inhabitants continue to dominate demographically even if they have little political or economic control.

Traditional people Those who follow a traditional way of life.

EPILOGUE TO SECTION 1

In the foregoing chapters, the impacts of economic development and other agents of cultural, community, and environmental change were discussed. A major emphasis is that although many benefits derive from such efforts, they might also lead to social and psychological dysfunction.

A key to understanding this phenomenon is the concept of anomie: a state of confusion, alienation, and disenfranchisement that occurs when change comes so quickly that people have trouble adapting and coping. Under some situations, people and communities become dysfunctional as a result of anomie, while on other occasions they adapt in positive and constructive ways.

By exploring anomie and how various kinds of populations (such as mainstream indigenous, Native, and traditional peoples as well as Third World and Fourth World people) deal with anomie, the stage is set to further explore the relationship between economic and social development and psychological dysfunction.

SECTION 2

Psychological perspectives

PROLOGUE TO SECTION 2

Building upon the discussions of anomie presented in Section 1, Section 2 discusses representative models for dealing with psychological dysfunction triggered by social and/or economic change. These discussions are representative, not exhaustive; many other approaches could be discussed.

Initially, in Chapter 6, the theory of anomie is employed as a model that can be adapted for discussions of change and dysfunction. Emile Durkheim's focus upon distinctive ethnic groups, along with Robert Merton typology of responses to anomie, creates the foundation of a useful model.

Building upon this general background, specific theories are analyzed. In Chapter 7, trauma is discussed in terms of cultural loss. Distinctive ethnic groups experiencing rapid change are potentially impacted when people are emotionally unable to confront hurtful events such as profound fears and losses. Not adequately dealing with disruptive change is one example of this response.

Theories regarding PTSD are initially discussed and merged with the concept of learned helplessness which occurs when people passively fail to avoid hurtful situations. Self-efficacy, in contrast, suggests that people can gain the belief that they can control their destiny. This attitude can be a strong, mitigating force that helps people overcome dysfunction that has been triggered by social and economic change and the resulting trauma.

Chapter 8 deals with Terror Management Theory, which maintains that people fear their inevitable death, and if this dread is not mitigated, psychological dysfunction can result. A strong cultural heritage, however, can reassure people by providing the belief that a part of them will live on after they die. When the future of the culture is in doubt, however, people can no longer take comfort that their

60 Psychological perspectives

heritage will remain. This ambivalence can increase the potential for psychological dysfunction.

Thus, starting with the concept of anomie, a variety of methods for discussing change and psychological dysfunction can be developed. A representative sample is discussed in Section 2.

6

THE STANDARD ANOMIE MODEL

Learning objectives

The concept of and the resulting stress, bewilderment, and pain are major causes of psychological dysfunction. In this chapter, various responses to anomie are analyzed (1) to understand their power and (2) to better perceive strategies for dealing with, reducing, and/or mitigating their negative potentials. By doing so, insights regarding dysfunction are discussed.

Specific issues addressed include:

(1) Understanding why the structural/functional method needs to be adjusted when working with indigenous, ethnic, and rural people.
(2) Appreciating how Merton's thinking can model the relationship between change and psychological dysfunction.
(3) Examining the various responses to anomie that Merton envisions and their relevance to the situations faced by indigenous, ethnic, and rural people.
(4) The potential positive and negative ramifications and implications of these responses.
(5) Recognizing specific ways to prevent and/or mitigate psychological dysfunction using these orientations as a foundation.

Introduction

As discussed in earlier chapters, the concept of anomie seeks to demonstrate the relationship between psychological dysfunction and disruptive economic and/or social change. Emile Durkheim's seminal work, for example, emphasizes how changing and transforming influences (such as the Industrial Revolution) led to higher rates of dysfunction among rural and ethnic enclaves.

62 Psychological perspectives

Building upon Durkheim's pioneering work, Robert Merton (1938, 1968) focused upon mainstream people who are unable or unwilling to live up to the standards of their society/culture (that is depicted as relatively stable and homogeneous). Doing so, of course, departed from Durkheim's work, which riveted upon distinctive groups, not a homogeneous community. As a result of this difference, Merton's orientation was not designed to deal with indigenous, ethnic, and rural peoples that are distinct from the dominant cultural milieu into which they were thrust.

In this regard, it is useful to remember that Merton was a structural/functionalist who viewed society using the analogy of a living organism. The bodies of animals, for example, are complex entities made up of interdependent parts that operate in unified and coordinated ways to advance the collective good. The heart pumps blood, the brain directs action, the muscles provide movement, and so forth. Each part contributes to the whole in a specific, positive, and coordinated manner. Organisms are synergistic: they are more than the mere sum of their parts. Structural/functionalists use an organic analogy or metaphor when envisioning society. In many situations, doing so is useful and appropriate.

Merton noticed, however, that although the structural/functional model suggests harmony and stability, under certain conditions, tensions arise between competing parts of this collective and cooperating social entity. When this occurs, teamwork and collaboration can break down, leading to dysfunction, crime, and deviance. The structural/functional paradigms of Merton's era, however, were ill-equipped to deal with such potentials. To correct this problem, Merton reformulated Durkheim's vision of anomie in ways that explore why some people fail to act in socially acceptable ways, violate cultural norms, cease to advance the collective good, and so forth.

Merton's goal was to update the structural/functional method in ways that acknowledge that some people fail to embrace and fulfill their assigned roles in the normal and expected manner. Nevertheless, Merton continued to envision society as relatively homogenous and stable.

The situation of many indigenous, ethnic, and rural peoples, however, is more complex than this. Although many of these people and their communities have been merged with or absorbed by a larger and more powerful entity, they might remain distinct from it. Many people who fail to conform to established norms are not mainstream people who "drifted away" from their society. Just the opposite: what is normal and acceptable within the larger, dominant culture or community might be abnormal and stressful for members of distinctive subgroups. As a result, these people might act in ways that, while deviant according mainstream standards, are normal for them.

Conversely, what is normal and natural for the mainstream might be alien and stressful when members of distinctive subgroups are forced to adhere to such alien and, perhaps, unwelcome standards of behavior. When people are unable to act and live in a manner that reflects their heritage, anomie and dysfunctional behavior are likely results.

As indicated earlier, Emile Durkheim clearly addressed this issue in his theory of anomie by consciously dealing with distinctive minorities, who typically came from rural or hinterland communities. Merton, in contrast, focused upon members of homogeneous communities who, lacking other opportunities, turn to crime and deviant behavior to correct this imbalance.

Merton emphasized that certain people find themselves at a disadvantage when attempting to satisfy culturally accepted goals in a legitimate manner. The resulting frustration and lack of conventional and sanctioned prospects can lead people to embrace some of society's norms while simultaneously rejecting others. Merton pointed to this tendency as a primary cause of deviance and/or criminal behavior.

Such issues, of course, raise the question of what frame of reference should be employed when analyzing particular cultural groups. Many sociologists, such as Merton, focus upon society at large. But if a distinctive community or subculture is the individual's primary reference or cohort group, that reality needs to be recognized. This can be relevant when patterns of dysfunction are being analyzed. This monograph embraces such an approach.

Merton's lasting significance

As discussed in Chapter 2, one of Merton's great contributions is developing a typology of responses to anomie. The somewhat truncated description provided in my earlier chapter is expanded here to operationalize the concept when applied to examples of dysfunction among distinctive social groups and their members. In doing so, Merton analyzed five distinct ways to respond to anomie, including: (1) Conformity, (2) Innovation, (3) Ritualization, (4) Retreatism, and (5) Rebellion (Merton 1968). A "refreshing" overview is provided here as a courtesy to the reader:

> *Conformity* involves people embracing the goals of the community as well as seeking to achieve these objectives in a manner that is socially acceptable. Conformity is a conservative response that preserves traditional relationships between people. Because it embraces traditional goals, methods, and solutions, however, conformity might not be a particularly effective method when people need to adapt to new challenges and conditions.
>
> *Innovation* takes place when people continue to embrace the traditional goals of society but achieve these objectives using unsanctioned methods that might violate cultural norms. Although doing so might involve criminal or antisocial behavior, it can also occur when indigenous, ethnic, and rural people act in unorthodox ways that offer economic, social, or cultural advances. When this is the case, innovation can ultimately contribute to cultural preservation, even if it initially generates tension or goes against the grain of the culture and community.
>
> *Ritualization* occurs when a person acts according to the norms of society in a rote and routine manner with little concern or attention to the goals that

64 Psychological perspectives

are sought. Tradition serves as a guide to behavior without an adequate focus upon the costs vs. benefits of adhering to its demands. Doing so can easily generate hurtful results because these actions are not likely to be performed for strategic or tactical reasons. When people act in a traditional manner, even though doing so is obviously counterproductive, the end result tends to be hurtful.

Retreatism arises when a person rejects both the cultural goals and the socially acceptable methods for achieving them without embracing any positive or beneficial alternative. These people are cut off from the beneficial influences of their heritage while simultaneously failing to embrace any positive alternatives. Merton observes that under such conditions, the potential for dysfunctional reactions, such as alcohol abuse, increases. When under the influence of alcohol or drugs, for example, the individual might be temporarily distracted from the plight faced, but fail to respond to the circumstances in a productive manner.

Rebellion occurs when a person (1) rejects both the goals that society provides and the traditional means of achieving them, while (2) simultaneously embracing substitutes that replace them. The old ways are rejected and new alternatives are embraced. When this occurs, profound changes of thought and attitude take place, although chaos might result. Different cultural factions might arise in conflict with one another. The situation created by widespread rebellion can be particularly painful to those who hold on to tradition and/or fear change.

Each of these responses to anomie is discussed.

Conformity

People typically conform to their traditions and do what is expected of them. This orthodox behavior often continues to dominate during the early phases of significant social and economic change. In some cases, it endures indefinitely. Conformists remain rooted in their traditions and heritage; as a result, they continue to embrace the established and long-standing mores of their culture as well as the strategies for achievement that are provided by it.

If subsistence hunting or slash and burn agriculture is the cultural norm and preferred profession, for example, conformists might follow that vocation even if more productive alternatives are available. Although the ability to be "successful" might become unlikely, conformists might adhere to their cultural ideals, even if doing so is "impractical".

These people tend to lose when new options displace the old. Achievements that might have previously earned respect become passé. This can result in sorrow, alienation, and psychological dysfunction for conformists who fail to adapt.

Conformists, however, might be able to serve vital cultural roles. Communities often embrace those who provide a living link with the past. Others might find

The standard anomie model **65**

a way to employ their old way of life by adapting it to serve new purposes. Thus, many Athabascan (Alaska Native Culture) men work as firefighters. In doing so, the teamwork that they have long used in subsistence life is rechanneled for use in another vocation that is currently in demand.

Other people might be able to continue in the old way (such as continuing a subsistence lifestyle) or pursuing traditional methods of farming. Thus, the Maya of the Toledo District of Belize (Central America) grow cacao in the traditional manner and sell it as "organic grown" at a premium price. By doing so, they are able to maintain their lifestyle while producing a cash crop in a manner that is not culturally disruptive.

In other situations, unfortunately, people who suffer from anomie continue to conform to traditional standards, even when doing so works against their best interest. Such people can set themselves up for continued failure and marginalization. Clinging to the past can prevent the acceptance of needed adjustments. Doing so might temporarily prevent the negative aspects of anomie, but merely postpone the inevitable; in the long run, doing so can make their pain and suffering even greater.

Thus, conformity is a conservative response that preserves traditional relationships between people. Although continuing to embrace tradition might temporarily reduce alienation, it might also prevent needed adaptation to new conditions. In some cases, nonetheless, it might be a viable option. Aspects of conformity are depicted in Table 6–1.

TABLE 6–1 Conformity

Issue	Description	Analysis
A choice	People continue acting in a conventional or orthodox manner.	Traditional folk behavior and beliefs dominate thought and action.
Possible benefits	Link to past and traditions. Less cultural loss. Less cultural stress. Possibly a viable choice.	Maintaining a link to tradition can reduce alienation and anomie. Might continue as a productive strategy.
Possible deficits	Conformists often fail to adapt to new circumstances.	Being overly connected with the past can prevent the embrace of productive alternatives.
Tradeoffs	Short-term lack of anomie might result in long-term alienation and inability to compete.	In the short term, conformity might reduce psychological dysfunction and cause problems later on.

DISCUSSION

Conformists are rooted in the mores of their culture that might provide psychological comfort and reduce anomie, especially in the short term. Although conformist behavior might be viable, if significant changes are ignored, unmitigated future problems can arise.

66 Psychological perspectives

Conformity, therefore, can both contribute to mental health and undermine it. By conforming, people remain connected to a heritage that is often comforting and can lessen anomie and its hurtful impacts. If conformity prevents or postpones people from adequately adjusting to inevitable change, long-term damage can result because those who conform to tradition might not be adequately prepared for the future.

Innovation

In conformity, people embrace their culture, its recommendations, and tactics. Because people are not asked to act in contradiction to their heritage, they will not face anomie and alienation due to conflicts with or a rejection of their heritage. Conformity, however, might prevent these people from effectively responding to challenges that need to be confronted.

In response to situations where conformity will not be effective, people often reject some of their traditional goals or methods of achieving these goals with more appropriate alternatives. By making relevant adjustments in thought and action, some pressures related to anomie might be relieved. Because doing so is at odds with their way of life, however, various triggers of anomie can arise.

Merton describes innovation as a situation in which the person maintains the goals of society, but alters the method of achieving these goals in order to be more efficient, effective, or to better cope with the circumstances encountered. Merton typically discussed innovation with reference to criminal behavior. An individual, for example, might embrace the goals of society (such as material success) but not be able to achieve this goal in a legal manner. As an alternative, a clandestine, but lucrative, alternative might be embraced.

Innovation, therefore, takes place when people continue to seek the traditional goals of society, but do so using unconventional methods that might violate cultural norms. Although this choice might involve criminal or antisocial behavior, it can also entail acting contrary to the established rules of society in a manner that ultimately leads to positive economic, social, or cultural advances. When such positive results occur, innovation can contribute to cultural preservation even when tensions arise or it challenges some of the underpinnings of society result.

As discussed earlier regarding the early 19th-century Iroquois Indians, farming had long been viewed as an inappropriate and shameful profession for men. The prophet Handsome Lake, however, taught that farming was an acceptable and manly profession and he encouraged his people to act accordingly. Handsome Lake's half-brother, who came to be known as Cornplanter, was a great warrior who used his new name to emphasize that "real men" could be farmers. Over time, Iroquois men accepted farming as a legitimate profession and this transition helped the culture to rebound.

Although this innovation was a break with the past, it helped to stabilize and revitalize Iroquois culture. This is a classic example of innovation that serves a positive role and is not criminal or antisocial in nature. Indeed, the adoption of

The standard anomie model **67**

TABLE 6–2 Innovation

Issue	Description	Analysis
Characteristics	The goals of society remain intact; the means of achieving them change.	Cultures provide both goals and methods. If methods change, goals can remain constant.
Adjustments	If old ways of achieving goals become passé, innovations provide a means of adjustment.	Although methods might change, continuity can survive in other areas. This can temper anomie and alienation.
Preservation	Although the acceptable methods of achieving goals might change, the objectives of society can remain intact.	The essence of the culture, its mores, goals, and aspirations remain, creating a degree of cultural, social, and psychic stability.
Benefits	Important aspects of the culture survive although other changes respond to evolving conditions.	Because part of their heritage survives, the amount of anomie and disruption people face is limited.

DISCUSSION

Cultures and the circumstances they face change over time. Cultures and people need mechanisms to adjust to emerging situations. Innovation provides that option; it can give rise to positive adjustments capable of lessening anomie and reducing psychological dysfunction.

this innovation has been credited with helping Iroquois culture return to stability and preventing the demise of the culture.

An overview of Innovation is presented in Table 6–2.

Innovation, therefore, can be a positive and productive means of reducing anomie and the psychological dysfunction associated with it. Examples of innovations (such as the early 19th-century Iroquois Indians) demonstrate the usefulness of this response and how it can contribute to cultural stability and good mental health.

Ritualization

Thus, innovation involves the adoption of methods that more effectively achieve socially acceptable goals. Doing so, however, might not initially mesh well with the culture. As a result, innovation might be disruptive in some ways even if it provides positive alternatives that are beneficial, help people cope, and serve as beneficial adaptations.

Ritualization involves continuing to embrace the culture merely as an end in itself. When this occurs, people might realize that their actions are futile, but continue anyway. Before Handsome Lake began to adapt Iroquois culture to mesh with changing times, for example, many Iroquois men continued to evaluate themselves according to the standards of the hunter and warrior. By the late 18th century, however, attempting to follow this way of life was fruitless and impossible. Nevertheless,

68 Psychological perspectives

many Iroquois men continued to follow this path even though doing so was pointless and counterproductive. These men chose to ritualistically embrace codes of behavior that were out of touch with the times. The result was suffering for themselves, their families, and for the greater Iroquois community.

Thus, ritualization can result in effort, energy, and hope being deployed in unproductive ways that end in disappointment and failure. From an emotional point of view, furthermore, those who ritualize are likely to set themselves up for underachievement and loss. These experiences can trigger a wide array of psychological dysfunctions.

Ritualization involves embracing tradition as a guide to behavior without an adequate focus upon the costs vs. the benefits of doing so. Under such circumstances, the ultimate goals of behavior are not taken into account as the conventions of action emerge as ends in themselves.

Those who embrace ritualization abandon strategic thinking that can lead to success in order to live by archaic standards. Doing so reduces effectiveness and is a recipe for failure and disaster.

Table 6–3 portrays Ritualization and its implications.

Ritualization, therefore, is a situation where people refuse to choose productive methods. The goals of the culture, however, remain. As a result, people continue to embrace passé methods in a changing world. Pain, suffering, and dysfunction can result.

TABLE 6–3 Ritualization

Issue	Description	Analysis
Characteristics	Cultural traditions are preserved in ways that prevent positive adjustments.	Rigid and unyielding choices prevent productively adapting to change.
Wasted energy	Those who follow unproductive paths waste time and energy that could be more fruitfully deployed.	Cultures facing stress need effective strategies instead of wasting time, effort, and resources on passé alternatives.
Emotional pain	If the old ways are counterproductive, following them can cause pain and disappointment.	Failure is painful. Being unproductive is painful. Ritualists set themselves up to experience increased suffering.
Dysfunction	The pain and suffering caused by non-productive strategies can trigger social and psychological dysfunction.	The end result of pain and suffering caused by ritualization is likely to be dysfunction.

DISCUSSION

Ritualization can prevent people from embracing strategies and tactics that potentially help individuals and communities survive and compete. When individuals and communities fail, psychological dysfunction can easily result.

Retreatism

Up until now, the people discussed have continued to embrace all (or at least a part) of their cultural heritage. As a result, some sort of continuity remains as a ballast or stabilizing force that tempers the impacts of change. The last two categories of response to be discussed ("retreatism" and "rebellion"), however, involve the relationships with cultures, heritages, and traditions being severed or eliminated. In retreatism, both society's goals and methods of achieving them are rejected, but no alternatives take their place. In rebellion, new methods and goals replace the old. In both cases, the connections with the old ways (as well as the comfort and stability they once provided) are abandoned.

Retreatism arises when a person rejects both the cultural goals and the socially acceptable methods for achieving them without embracing any positive or beneficial alternative. These people are cut off from the positive influences of their heritage and no alternatives or compensation for the loss is sought or embraced. Merton emphasized that dysfunctional behavior, such as alcohol abuse, can easily increase under such circumstances. While under the influence of alcohol or drugs, for example, the victim of retreatism might be temporarily distracted from the plight faced, but fail to respond in an effective manner.

Retreatists tend to lack a social grounding and/or mission in life. As a result, these people are apt to be aimless and alienated. This condition, of course, can easily lead to dysfunction. Retreatism is outlined in Table 6–4.

TABLE 6–4 Retreatism

Issue	Description	Analysis
Characteristics	The methods and goals of society are rejected but not replaced.	Retreatists tend to lack a roadmap for life and a model to live by.
Alienation	People exist without a compass or greater purpose due to a lack of belief and commitment.	Not directed by a viable system of belief or commitment, social connections and responsibilities can atrophy.
Little comfort	Possessing no stabilizing force or belief system, people find little comfort in life.	Without a social system and belief structure to rely upon, important sources of comfort and stability are eliminated.
Potential for dysfunction	Cut off from meaningful perspective or beliefs, the seeds for psychological dysfunction exist.	When people believe in nothing and have no established goals, sorrow and dysfunction can easily arise.

DISCUSSION

Retreatism, therefore, is a complete rejection of the beliefs, mores, and methods that society provides. Without this grounding, the emotional supports needed to prevent psychological dysfunction are weakened.

70 Psychological perspectives

Retreatism, therefore, can be a fertile ground for psychological dysfunction because the coping mechanisms provided by society are no longer functioning. No alternative, furthermore, fills the void experienced by these individuals. Psychological dysfunction emerges as a likely possibility.

Rebellion

Retreatism is negative. It is based purely upon rejection and it does not involve the establishment or embrace of positive alternatives. Retreatism simply rejects, leaving a gap that can be a source of alienation and dysfunction. In rebellion, in contrast, the individual rejects tradition while simultaneously replacing what has been lost or abandoned.

Rebels, therefore, have a vision that can help them to psychologically position themselves within a new emotional, social, and ethical framework. Nevertheless, rebels abandon both the established methods and the goals of their culture.

Looked at from this general perspective, rebels might adopt the methods and goals of intrusive outsiders as replacements for their heritage and traditions. In an earlier chapter, for example, we talked about Chinua Achebe's novel *No Longer at Ease* (1969). The story, as you might recall, concerns Obi Oknokwo, a young indigenous leader who had been trained at a Western university, speaks perfect English, and dresses in the Western style. He clearly rejects his traditions, hobnobs as a sophisticate, and is at odds with the desires of his parents. Caught between two cultures, however, he faces alienation and sorrow as a result of the conflicts between the new life he embraces and the old one he has discarded. He is a good example of rebels who suffer when they venture beyond their culture and its way of life.

In addition to his work regarding anomie, Robert Merton also called attention to what he called the "reference group", a term that depicts those who the individual refers to when choosing role models and/or selecting strategies of life, methods of achievement, as well as evaluating personal success or failure. In the case of Obi Oknokwo, his dominant reference groups are the colonial minority and the outside world.

Thus, rebellion can occur when people (1) reject both the goals that society provides and the established or conventional methods for achieving them, while (2) simultaneously accepting substitutes for both. When profound changes of thought and attitude take place, chaos, suffering, and agony might result.

Different factions within the culture or community, furthermore, might arise in conflict with one another, causing strife and disorder. The situation created by widespread rebellion can be particularly painful to those who cling to tradition and/or fear change. Rebellion can also cause inner tension within people who follow its path.

Although they might experience alienation, however, rebels are not prone to feel pain and dysfunction due to a lack of belief. On the contrary, they are likely to feel that they are members of a wave of the future. If their rebellion fails or proves

The standard anomie model **71**

TABLE 6–5 Rebellion

Issue	Description	Analysis
Characteristics	People embrace both new goals, and new methods for achieving them.	An alternative to retreatism, rebellion provides new alternatives.
New focus	The old ways are replaced. Doing so provides people with a new focus and something to believe in.	New goals and strategies can be more productive, on the one hand, and disruptive and alienating, on the other.
Cultural tension	Rebellion can set up tension between adherents and other factions within the community.	When the mores of a culture are overtly challenged, tensions are likely to develop.
Potential for dysfunction	Those who are displaced by the successes of the rebels can suffer. The failure of the rebellion can lead to dysfunction among its adherents.	The act of rebellion can cause dysfunction among both traditionalists and rebels. Both potentials need to be recognized.

DISCUSSION

In rebellion, both the goals of society and the means of achieving them are replaced. Although positive in some respects, rebellion can lead to tensions within both traditionalisms and rebels.

not to be viable, however, anomie, sorrow, and dysfunction may result. Table 6–5 provides an overview of rebellion.

Rebellion, therefore, is the last of an array of possible responses that were outlined by Robert Merton. Although other theorists and practitioners envision their own expanded typologies, Merton's observation that a range of options exist is useful. As a result, Merton's basic approach is a permanent contribution, even if later researchers seek to fine-tune his work.

An array of options

Merton's typology provides a wide variety of ways in which people respond to rapid change and the possibility of anomie. Some reactions to anomie result in positive adaptation, while others lead to dysfunction and counterproductive choices.

Although other social scientists have developed typologies that are more complex than Merton's and possess additional categories, they tend to follow Merton's strategy of envisioning a range of reactions, how they differ from each other, and their implications regarding deviance and dysfunction. This basic approach can be very useful to social planners, practitioners, and those who seek to mitigate possible problems associated with change. With these uses in mind, Table 6–6

72 Psychological perspectives

TABLE 6–6 A Typology of Responses

Category	Description	Analysis
Conformity	Established goals and methods remain.	Maintaining traditions provides continuity, but doing so can prevent needed adaptation.
Innovation	Goals are kept, methods are changed.	Goals provide continuity, new methods allow for healthy response to change.
Ritualization	Preserve methods, ignore goals.	Acting in an appropriate manner is an end in itself. Goals of the culture get little attention.
Retreatism	Reject both goals and methods; no replacements.	Traditions abandoned, no alternative embraced. People cut off from meaningful aspects of life.
Rebellion	Replace both goals and are methods.	Embrace new goals and methods can be positive, but might lead to disruptive divisions in society.

DISCUSSION

An array of options exists as cultures respond to changing conditions. Some potentially lead to dysfunction while others might provide relief. These options need to be recognized and addressed.

portrays these alternatives in a manner of value to individuals, communities, and decision makers.

By being aware of these categories (or parallel methods), those involved with social and economic change can begin to understand a fuller range of responses in order to (1) mitigate hurtful ramifications, as well as (2) taking advantage of their benefits. By doing so, psychological dysfunction can be more effectively predicted and mitigated.

Discussion

The concept of anomie is invaluable when analyzing how social and economic change can trigger psychological dysfunction. As originally formulated by Emile Durkheim, the theory of anomie was designed to deal with ethnic enclaves facing crises that were caused by powerful, intrusive forces. These are exactly the types of pressures that contemporary indigenous, ethnic, and rural people face.

Building upon Durkheim, Robert Merton envisions a number of responses to anomie. By doing so, a variety of ways in which people respond to profound changes are identified. By evaluating particular situations with reference to this expanded view of anomie and its implications, social planners, practitioners, communities, and individuals can better understand the pressures faced and how to effectively deal with them.

Discussion questions

(1) Robert Merton reformulated the theory of anomie in order to fit the needs of structural/functional sociology. Why might this hinder efforts to deal with ethnic enclaves? Why might Durkheim's work be more useful in this regard?

(2) How can Merton's thinking effectively deal with the relationship between change and psychological dysfunction? Focus upon the range of categories of potential response that Merton acknowledges. Why is this useful and helpful?

(3) Merton was a strong advocate of the structural/functional method and he developed his model of anomie in order to account for change within a paradigm that encouraged cooperation. Could this adjustment keep the approach from dealing with distinct people?

(4) How can the theory of anomie be adjusted to deal with people who are not a typical part of a homogeneous society? How can misreading groups and/or society in terms of perceived homogeneity lead to poor analysis and strategy? Discuss with an example of your choice.

(5) Preventing and/or mitigating psychological dysfunction should be a major goal of projects involving social and economic change. How can an understanding of anomie facilitate such initiatives? Provide an example.

References

Achebe, C. (1969). *No Longer at Ease*. (London: Heinemann).

Merton, R. K. (1938). "Social Structure and Anomie." *American Sociological Review* 3 (5): 672–682.

Merton, R. K. (1968). *Social Structure and Social Theory*. (New York: Free Press; Other additions: 1949 and 1957).

Relevant terms

Anomie   A state of confusion and normlessness in which people no longer understand the situations they face, leading to sorrow and dysfunction.

Conformity   Merton's category of response in which both the goals of society and the means of achieving them continue to be embraced.

Crime   Acting in illegal ways. Merton connects crime to anomie.

Deviance   Failing to act according to cultural norms. Merton considers deviance to be an abnormal response to anomie.

Durkheim, Emile   Developed a theory of anomie that focused upon the stress of social change upon ethnic enclaves.

Homogeneity   All or most people acting in according to the norms of society. Structural/functionalists consider this to be normal.

Innovation   Merton's category of response in which the goals of society remain constant, but the means of achieving them change.

Merton, Robert   (1) Adapted anomie to deal with homogeneous communities and (2) provided a typology of responses to anomie.

Merton's typology   Different responses to anomie including conformity, innovation, retreatism, rebellion, and ritualization.

74 Psychological perspectives

Organic analogy Dealing with society as if it is a living being in which specific parts cooperate by providing specialized services in mutually beneficial ways.

Rebellion Merton's category of response in which both the goals of society and the means of achieving them are replaced.

Reference Group A group of people who serve as a frame of reference when people are evaluating themselves and/or their situations.

Retreatism A response to anomie in which people reject both the goals of society and the means of achieving them, but do not replace them.

Ritualization Merton's category of response in which people behave in a traditional manner even though they realize doing so will not be effective.

Structuralism/Functionalism A theory of society that tends to emphasize ongoing cooperative structures and a homogeneous population that tends to act according to cultural norms.

Subgroups Groups of people who do not fit the norm of the majority. Structural/functionalists deemphasize their significance.

7

IMPLICATIONS OF CULTURAL TRAUMA

Learning objectives

Trauma involves the impact of hurtful events upon people. If not adequately dealt with, dysfunction can occur. Theories of trauma can be merged with the concept of learned helplessness, a situation where people passively fail to avoid or escape hurtful situations. Self-efficacy, which occurs when people believe that they can control their destiny, can be a mitigating force helping people resist dysfunction associated with trauma. This chapter will:

(1) Introduce PTSD as a specific example of cultural stress and trauma.
(2) Discuss cultural trauma and its possible impacts upon people undergoing change.
(3) Understand learned helplessness and how it can control people subjected to profound change.
(4) Envision self-efficacy as an alternative to learned helplessness.
(5) Discuss overcoming learned helplessness using self-efficacy to cope with change.

Introduction

A basic theme of this monograph is that profound and unmitigated change can trigger anomie that involves feelings of doubt, hopelessness, and confusion. The resulting stress might initiate productive responses or adaptations, on the one hand, or social and psychological dysfunction, on the other.

Emile Durkheim (as discussed in earlier chapters) provided the seminal analysis of anomie. His work centers upon rural people from hinterland communities who experience a disorienting transition from small, intimate communities to a more impersonal, urban life, regimented wage labor, and so forth. Durkheim's emphasis upon cultural conflict and tension is especially useful when dealing with distinctive social groups.

76 Psychological perspectives

PTSD is a psychological dysfunction that typically involves people who have experienced great personal fear, danger, or loss and, as a result, exhibit abnormal degrees of anxiety and/or counterproductive responses. (For a general orientation regarding PTSD see Cash 2006.) Battle-weary soldiers, rape victims, car crash survivors, and so forth commonly receive this diagnosis. Due to the fact that PTSD is usually associated with fear and physical danger, those subjected to cultural change and tensions might not appear to be experiencing PTSD.

PTSD is one response to hurtful pressures. Others exist, and collectively they can be viewed as responses to trauma. In recent years, the Substance Abuse and Mental Health Services Administration of the United States (SAMHSA) has emphasized the role of trauma in mental illness and psychological dysfunction. The goal of this chapter is to adapt these insights to deal with cultural trauma. Other theories and methods are incorporated into this model as necessary. Because theories and therapy involving PTSD model have already dealt with the impacts of cultural change, this discussion begins with examples of that approach.

PTSD: an overview

For hundreds of years, there has been a recognition that people who have been subjected to horrific events are likely to exhibit dysfunctional behavior. Some of my therapist friends, for example, have told me that a scene involving Lady Percy that appears in the second act of Shakespeare's *Henry IV Part 1* (written in 1597) provides an accurate description of PTSD. During and after World War I, the term "shell shock" was used to identify those who had become psychologically incapacitated due to their battle experiences. Over the years, phrases such as "soldier's heart" have been used to describe dysfunctions that result from the horror of battle.

After the Vietnam War, many veterans of the conflict were treated for psychological trauma that was related to their military careers. In the process, a wide array of research projects addressed the relationship between dangerous military experiences and mental illness. Eventually, the term PTSD was developed to identify dysfunction that had been triggered by the stress of danger, fear, and loss. This formal description of this condition was included in the Third Edition (1980) of the *Diagnostic and Statistical Manual of Mental Disorders* (*DSM*) [the definitive listing/typology of mental dysfunction published by the American Psychological Association, now in its Fifth Edition]. PTSD continues to be recognized as a psychological disorder in this definitive reference work.

An authoritative and detailed description of PTSD (as currently understood) is available in the Fifth Edition of the *DSM* (2013). Located in the "Anxiety Disorders" chapter of the Fourth Edition of the *DSM* (*DSM-IV*), PTSD is currently included in a new chapter entitled "Stressor-Related Disorders". The reader is urged to consult this important reference work to gain a broader understanding of the malady and how it is currently envisioned. Due to the limitations of space, only a bare overview is presented here.

PTSD is a disorder triggered by stress and the anxiety related to it. People who receive a diagnosis of PTSD develop their symptoms after experiencing a traumatic

Implications of cultural trauma **77**

event; commonly occurring symptoms include a tendency for people to avoid thinking about or coming in contact with anything that reminds them of their disturbing experience. In addition, people suffering from PTSD might experience amnesia regarding events that trigger the condition. Although afflicted individuals often avoid thinking and talking about the cause of their suffering, memories are likely to crop up involuntarily as flashbacks or nightmares. "Acute" episodes of PTSD last for less than three months. If they continue longer than that, the case is categorized as "chronic". In some instances, the symptoms emerge a considerable time after the traumatic event. On other occasions, they begin soon after.

Originally, a diagnosis of PTSD was typically given to people who had experienced trauma due to military combat. As time has gone on, the use of PTSD has been expanded to deal with a broader range of situations. The root cause of the diagnosis, however, is usually traced to violence, danger, and loss. Typical triggers suggested by HelpGuide.org (a layman-oriented information website provided in cooperation with Harvard University) include natural disasters, car or plane crashes, terrorist attacks, sudden death of a loved one, rape, kidnapping, assault, sexual or physical abuse, and childhood neglect.

HelpGuide goes on to observe: "Traumatic events are more likely to cause PTSD when they involve a severe threat to . . . life or personal safety: the more extreme and prolonged the threat, the greater the risk of developing PTSD. . . . The extent to which the traumatic event was unexpected, uncontrollable, and inescapable also plays a role". Thus, even when expanded beyond military issues, the descriptions of PTSD tend to focus upon violence and physical danger.

In tabular form, PTSD is analyzed in Table 7–1.

TABLE 7–1 PTSD: An Overview

Issue	Description	Analysis
Causes	Danger, fear, and loss.	Conventional applications center around physical danger and/or the fear of it, coupled with possible accompanying loss.
Original uses	Analyzing and treating those who have suffered the horror of war and battle.	The standard conception of PTSD is largely based upon research involving Vietnam veterans.
Expanded uses	Dealing with the impacts of fear, danger, and loss in other contexts such as abuse, rape, and accidents.	Although the use of PTSD has expanded in recent years, it is typically used to deal with those who have faced physical danger.
Extending PTSD	An expanded use of the PTSD diagnosis involves trauma and loss other than physical danger.	Extending PTSD to deal with cultural losses can provide a method for dealing with traumatic social and cultural change.

DISCUSSION

PTSD typically focuses on physical violence and loss. As a result, it does not intuitively appear to be connected with cultural change. This gap needs to be addressed.

78 Psychological perspectives

PTSD, therefore, is a recognized psychological dysfunction. It is usually associated with people who have experienced great fear, danger, or loss. As a result, other people such as those experiencing cultural trauma without physical danger, have not typically been viewed in terms of PTSD.

Cultural PTSD

Earlier in this book we briefly analyzed the work of Harold Napoleon and the responses to anomie and cultural loss that he documents. Writing as an informed layman who personally experienced the pressures and dysfunctions he writes about, Napoleon's account is compelling, comes from the heart, and provides a first-hand account of the trauma faced by indigenous people experiencing traumatic change. In doing so, Napoleon used PTSD as an explanatory devise.

Napoleon's work documents how the Yup'ik people (an Alaska Native culture) faced losses and psychological assaults that were the catalyst for a high incidence of dysfunctional behavior, including widespread alcoholism and a general breakdown of society. Napoleon makes the case that this dysfunctional behavior closely parallels those who have been diagnosed with PTSD. Napoleon continues by suggesting that these events create a vicious circle because people who were already demoralized and dysfunctional faced increasingly hurtful situations (in part, perhaps, due to their own actions).

Many other indigenous, ethnic, and rural groups (some of which were discussed previously) have responded in a similar manner including Native Hawaiians Cash (2006) and Davis (1968) and the Maori of New Zealand (Gilgen 1996). Napoleon, adopting a model based on PTSD, clearly links the decline of his people (and the dysfunctional behavior that coincides with it) to the painful intrusions of outsiders and the changes and diseases that resulted from contact. Napoleon observes:

> When the first White men arrived . . . the [Yup'ik] people did not immediately abandon their old ways. It is an historical fact that they resisted Russian efforts to colonize them. . . . They were not impressed by the White men, even though they quickly adopted their technology and goods.
>
> *(Napoleon 1996, 9)*

White contact, however, eventually lead to a horrible crisis caused by disease. Napoleon tells us:

> The changes were brought about as a result of the introduction of diseases that had been born in the slums of Europe during the dark and middle ages, diseases carried by the traders, the whalers, and the missionaries. To these diseases, the Yup'ik and other Native tribes had no immunity and . . . they would lose up to 60% of their people. As a result of epidemics, the Yup'ik world would go upside down; it would end.
>
> *(Napoleon 1996, 9–10)*

Implications of cultural trauma   **79**

These epidemics, which occurred from time to time, culminated in the "Great Death" of 1900. "Out of the suffering, confusion, desperation, heartbreak, and trauma was born a new generation of Yup'ik people. They were born into shock. They woke to a world in shambles, many of their beliefs strewn around them, dead" (Napoleon 1996, 11).

Napoleon describes this situation in ways that closely resemble PTSD:

> The world the survivors woke to was without anchor. The *andalkug* [medicine men], their medicines, and their beliefs had all passed away overnight. They woke up to shock, listless, confused, bewildered, heartbroken, and afraid. Like soldiers on an especially gruesome battlefield, they were shell shocked. . . . Famine, starvation and disease resulting from the epidemic continued to plague them through the 1950s and many more perished. These were the people whom the missionaries would call wretched, lazy, even listless. Gone were the people who Nelson [early White explorer] so admired. The long night of suffering had begun for the survivors of the Great Death and their descendants.
>
> *(Napoleon 1996, 12–13)*

Thus, the demoralized situations that the Yup'ik faced were unprecedented and led to profound dysfunction that can be viewed as a variant of PTSD. This resulting legacy and pattern of dysfunction has been longstanding. Writing in the 1990s, Napoleon notes that even though material conditions had greatly improved for the Yup'ik, psychological dysfunction remained and the suicide rate was at epidemic levels. (That situation continues to the time of this writing, and shows no signs of abating among certain segments of Yup'ik society.)

Even though the Yup'ik experienced a particularly harsh fate, expanding and generalizing Harold Napoleon's observations is useful. By doing so, a model that can be called "Cultural PTSD" can be offered. So viewed, the observation can be made that a major cause of the dysfunction experienced by indigenous, ethnic, and rural people involves a sense of helplessness and hopelessness that has been triggered by hurtful contact with the outside world. As Napoleon demonstrates, this pain and dysfunction can persist even though physical and economic conditions are getting better and the quality of life experienced by people appears to be improving if conventional "social indicators" are used in the evaluation.

Although originally employed when dealing with victims of physical danger, therefore, PTSD can be expanded to include a variant that is centered around cultural losses, fears, dysfunctional responses, and so forth. This variation, that will be referred to as "Cultural PTSD", is abstracted in Table 7–2.

Cultural PTSD, therefore, can be used to deal with individuals and communities that face profound pressures stemming from cultural change and losses. It is intertwined with the type of dysfunction that Durkheim discussed in terms of unmitigated cultural change.

Even though Napoleon is not a trained psychologist or clinician, he provides a compelling analysis. Not being professionally trained, however, his use of PTSD

80 Psychological perspectives

TABLE 7–2 Cultural PTSD

Issue	Description	Analysis
Original	PTSD originally dealt with dysfunction caused by physical fear and loss.	Focusing on physical danger, cultural issues are not intuitively connected to PTSD.
Cultural variant	Cultures can impact mental health. People facing significant cultural attacks might respond in a manner resembling PTSD.	Even without physical danger, profound cultural losses can trigger dysfunction in ways that parallel PTSD. This potential needs to be recognized.
Expanded victims	Members of communities who are emotionally unprepared to deal with the stresses and changes impacting their culture.	In recent years, PTSD has been expanded to deal with an increased variety of people. Cultural PTSD is a legitimate and useful example of that trend.

DISCUSSION

Cultural PTSD represents a logical expansion of the diagnosis in order to deal with traumatic loss that is associated with cultural stress and decline. The work of Harold Napoleon demonstrates the viability of doing so. That approach is generalized and expanded here.

might be somewhat inaccurate even though it well communicates his message. As a result, the issues he addresses might be better expressed using broader conceptions of trauma that reflect the state of the art of psychology and therapy.

Expanding beyond PTSD

Although the Substance Abuse and Mental Health Services Administration of the United States (SAMHSA) often focuses upon trauma involving physical threats or perceived danger, it has devised a very general definition of trauma which states:

> Individual trauma results from an event, series of events, or set of circumstances that are experienced by an individual as physically or emotionally harmful or life threatening and that has lasting adverse effects on the individual's functioning and mental, physical, social, emotional, or spiritual well-being.
>
> *(SAMHSA 2014)*

In spite of the general nature of this definition, much attention is currently being directed towards specific issues such as the impact of trauma upon children. The Adverse Childhood Experiences (ACE) research program is prominent within this research stream (Felita et al. 1998). It observes "Adverse childhood experiences (ACEs) include verbal, physical, or sexual abuse, as well as family dysfunction. . . . ACEs have been linked to a range of adverse health outcomes in adulthood, including substance abuse, depression, cardiovascular disease, diabetes, cancer, and premature mortality" (Anonymous 2010).

Implications of cultural trauma **81**

Although this definition does not exclude or rule out cultural trauma, such events have received relatively little emphasis. Although dealing with these cultural issues is important and justified, relatively little attention has been directed towards studying the impact of cultural stress and loss upon indigenous, ethnic, and rural peoples experiencing significant change. A possible explanation for this lack of attention might be that these groups tend to be small and circumscribed minorities and, as a result, they have not attracted adequate attention.

A technique advocated by SAMHSA, however, is broad enough to deal with such cases. SAMHSA recommends dealing with trauma using what it calls the "3 Es model", which stands for "events", "experience", and "effect".

"Events" refers to what in particular happened to the person, group, or community. For present purposes, the discussion centers around significant actions and changes that undercut the local cultural, traditions, ways of life, and so forth. These experiences, of course, may be connected to or amplified by other traumas. A number of questions can be asked in this regard. What kind of change is taking place? How rapid is it? Is (or was) the change mitigated in a meaningful manner? And so forth.

The fact that events and trends are transforming the culture and/or people's relationship to it, however, does not necessarily make the actual "experience" traumatic (as they are perceived by people). Much cultural change and/or technological borrowings, for example, are welcomed, useful, and not overly disruptive. In Alaska, for example, the initial introduction of Western goods, such as iron cooking kettles, firearms, and so forth, were quickly and gratefully accepted by indigenous peoples who lived outside the sphere of colonial influence. Cultural diffusion and new trading relationships did not cause stress, hardship, or trauma among these people. As a result, such innovations were quickly embraced by the people and phased into the pre-existing way of life in positive and constructive ways.

Not all change, however, proceeds under such stress-free and trauma-free circumstances. Many Alaska Natives who lived under the control of intruders from Russian and the United States, for example, suffered grievously. Thus, particular events need to be evaluated with attention as to how they are experienced by communities and/or individuals. The events and how they are experienced are distinctive phenomena and not to be confused with each other.

"Effect" refers to the actual results of the experiences and events. When evaluating the effect, a number of questions can be asked. How did they contribute to the life of the people, both for the better and worse? What problems or benefits emerged? And so forth. By dealing with the influence of events, not merely the events themselves, the full effect can be better envisioned.

Various tools such as the Revised Life Stressor Checklist provide a means of assessing if people should be viewed as victims needing treatment for dysfunctions such as PTSD (Norris and Hamblen 2004). Although these tools are valuable and needed, they are not designed to deal with cultural stress and trauma.

Although the discussion above is a very truncated overview, it demonstrates the expanded and broadened way in which trauma is understood. A tabular view is presented in Table 7–3.

82 Psychological perspectives

TABLE 7–3 Trauma: An Expanded View

Issue	Analysis
Trauma	Physically and/or emotionally harmful. Lasting effects result.
3 Es model	A three-fold model of trauma that examines the event, how the event was experienced, and the overall effect.
Event	The actual event that may or may not have been traumatic.
Experience	How people experience the event. What people felt, thought, and other relevant implications. These factors determine if trauma was experienced.
Effect	The results and influences caused by the event and its experience. In truly traumatic events, significant and long-term negative consequences result.
Life Stressor Checklist	When dealing with trauma, assessment tools are very useful. One example is the Life Stressor Checklist. This commonly used tool, however, was not designed to deal with indigenous, ethnic, and rural people facing significant trauma due to cultural change, weakening traditions, or personal alienation from their heritage.

DISCUSSION

Although trauma is increasingly viewed in a broad manner, the actual tools used to assess and deal with it appear to concentrate upon issues facing the mainstream population. These tools can be usefully supplemented with techniques that better assess and serve indigenous, ethnic, and rural people.

Culturally aware conceptualizations of trauma, therefore, are able to deal with the particular situations typically faced by indigenous, ethnic, and rural people. One way of doing so is to combine the tools used with PTSD and trauma therapy with the concept of "learned helplessness".

Learned helplessness

B. F. Skinner was a behavioral psychologist who conditioned animals in order to influence their behavior in specific ways. The method Skinner used is commonly referred to as Operant Conditioning. In general, Skinner studied how the experiences that animals receive can increase the likelihood that they will respond in particular ways. In other words, Skinner analyzed how animals could be trained to respond in a predictable manner.

In a hypothetical experiment reminiscent of Skinner, the researcher might provide food to an animal when a certain task is performed (such as pushing a button with its nose). Thus, when a rat hits the button, food is dispensed. Although this required task will initially be performed accidently and randomly, eventually the rats realize the connection between food and a certain action and, as a result, they gain control over the food supply. You might say the rats become empowered.

As time went on, Skinner became interested in applying what he had learned manipulating rats in order to make society run more smoothly. His novel,

Walden 2, for example, concerns a futuristic world that operates on principles suggested by behavioral psychology. In addition to appearing in fiction, ideas based on behavioral psychology have been adapted for use by mental health therapists and counselors. In general, behavioral techniques can be (and are) used to help people learn and, thereby, develop a greater degree of control over their lives (as well as guiding behavior in a socially acceptable manner). These goals are achieved by prompting people to make choices that more effectively control their destiny, instead of accepting a passive existence.

But what if animals (or people) are put in situations where they are taught that they have no control over their fate? Or if they come to believe that nothing they do will make any difference? That is the issue addressed by the work of Martin Seligman and Maier Steven (1965) and his theory of "learned helplessness".

In the 1960s, Seligman conducted an experiment in which dogs received electrical shocks after hearing a bell ring. The dogs, however, had no way to avoid the shock. Eventually, they gave up and accepted the pain as inevitable. Later, when the dogs were put in a position where they could avoid the shock (an escape route was provided), they shook with fear, but did nothing to avoid their pain because they had been conditioned to believe that their situation was helpless. The dogs remained fatalistic and passive even after they were given the power to control their destiny.

The same pattern of behavior that Seligman observed when studying his dogs might also occur among people who are forced to accept what the powerful demand. Under such circumstances, people can be conditioned to live, act, and believe that nothing they do can will change the undesirable situations they face.

Consider the Yup'ik that Harold Napoleon describes. Not only were these people subjected to forces that could not easily be challenged, the traditional means of coping (traditional economic system and cultural support) were ripped away. Many of these people gave up.

These victims, nevertheless, ultimately exhibited (1) something akin to PTSD or trauma, and (2) responses closely resembling learned helplessness.

Experiencing feelings of profound loss due to powerful forces leading to PTSD, people can easily conclude that they are powerless. In other words, they become passive and submissive. Doing so can lead people to give up and accept their situation even if doing so results in further dysfunction (such as substance abuse, suicide, and so forth). Just like the dogs that Seligman studied, if people give up, they can become fatalistic in their thought, passive in their inaction, and submissively continue to suffer. This can be true even if more positive alternatives exist. Thus, learned helpless has much in common with feelings of anomie that arise when people believe they cannot control or escape the changes in their lives. Table 7–4 explores these parallels.

This pattern appears to be replicated in many examples where people are exposed to massive outside change, including (and especially) indigenous, ethnic, and traditional people who live in developing regions. These people need to gain faith in their abilities to control their own destiny. In other words, they need to transcend learned helplessness. The concept of self-efficacy, associated with Albert Bandura, provides a means of doing so.

84 Psychological perspectives

TABLE 7–4 Learned Helplessness and Anomie

Issue	Description	Analysis
Learned helplessness	Past events lead to the belief that a person is helpless.	People who believe a situation is helpless will come to think and act accordingly.
Passive nature	People fatalistically accept the circumstances before them.	Under these circumstances, people will not try to improve their situation.
Possible dysfunction	Facing anxiety because they do not attempt to avoid a bad situation, people might become dysfunctional.	People facing an intolerable situation without hope of relief are prime candidates for dysfunction.
Parallels with anomie	Anomie involves people being unable to achieve acceptable goals in acceptable ways.	This potential response closely parallels the response to anomie in which people become dysfunctional.

DISCUSSION

Cultural helplessness and anomie largely reflect and duplicate each other. Both deal with the hurtful impacts of fatalism and the passive inaction that can result from it.

Self-efficacy: antidote for hopelessness

Self-efficacy refers to situations where people believe that they have a significant degree of control over their lives and the situations they face. It is the opposite of learned helplessness. The work of Albert Bandura is important in this regard.

Albert Bandura is a celebrated psychologist. Of humble origins, he was raised in rural Alberta, Canada. This environment provided Bandura with insights that aided his career and focused his attention in areas that are relevant for studying social change and psychological dysfunction, especially among rural people and ethnic enclaves.

Specifically, during the late 1940s, Bandura took a summer job working in the Canadian Yukon helping to maintain the Alaska Highway (that connects Alaska with Canada and the rest of the continental United States). The road had been quickly built as an emergency measure during World War II; after the conflict ended, the route needed constant repair and upgrading. When earning his summer money, young Bandura was exposed to the bawdy life of gambling and excessive drinking while in the Yukon. In many ways, this environment was probably similar to what Harold Napoleon had experienced; Napoleon's Yup'ik people live in the Yukon River watershed (although in Alaska, not the Canadian Yukon).

Eventually Bandura became interested in learning how people can come to believe in themselves, taking control of their destiny and thoughts. Since the 1970s, much of his work has been concerned with self-efficacy, a concept that was built upon social cognitive theory.

Bandura's work expands beyond social cognitive theory by envisioning self-efficacy as a situation where people believe that they can successfully achieve goals,

Implications of cultural trauma **85**

perform tasks, and so forth. Bandura also concludes that the degree to which people believe that they can accomplish something plays a significant role in what they do and how they act.

The concept of self-efficacy builds upon Bandura's social cognitive theories and employs his concept of "observational learning", which emphasizes that people's actions tend to replicate what they have seen in the past. The main concept in social cognitive theory is that people notice what others do and what occurs as a result. Thus, the degree to which a person exhibits self-efficacy (or not) is, in large part, an artifact of observations the individual has made and the conclusions that are drawn from this evidence. In other words, self-efficacy (or a lack of it) resonates from the individual's observations.

Ultimately, people who possess a high degree of self-efficacy believe they can succeed, do well, control their own destiny, and so forth. As a result, such people are more willing to accept a challenge than those who lack these optimistic feelings. Such opinions, furthermore, are based upon beliefs that stem from observation. These findings are abstracted in Table 7–5.

On many occasions, when indigenous, ethnic, and rural people are confronted with powerful outside forces, they experience loss. The resulting experiences can create a situation involving operational learning that leads people to believe that they cannot succeed. If this assessment becomes ingrained, people are likely to

TABLE 7–5 Self-efficacy

Issue	Description	Analysis
Observational learning	People make observations and draw conclusions from them.	Using a form of intuitive empiricism, beliefs are based on past experiences.
Self-efficacy	Self-efficacy is the belief that people have a degree of control over their lives.	If the observations people make indicate they can control their destiny, they develop a stronger sense of self-efficacy.
Cultural enclaves	Cultural groups facing stress and loss need examples of success to build feelings of self-efficacy.	Observational learning emphasizes the importance of concrete examples in establishing self-efficacy.
Reducing dysfunction	Self-efficacy can help build a sense of purpose and empowerment that can mitigate anomie and PTSD as well as lessening dysfunction.	Combined, anomie, PTSD, and learned helplessness suggest a lack of control. They can, however, be mitigated by self-efficacy in ways that reduce dysfunction.

DISCUSSION

The concept of self-efficacy is a key contribution of Albert Bandura. It emphasizes that behavior is largely an artifact of what people believe they can accomplish. The concept of observational learning points to the fact that people believe what they observe. In order for people to empower themselves, they need to see examples of success and control. Such examples can lead to self-efficacy.

86 Psychological perspectives

become passive (as we saw in the case of learned helplessness). Self-efficacy, however, involves people coming to believe in themselves and concluding that what they do can make a difference in their lives. By grooming people to experience a feeling of self-efficacy, the fatalism of learned helplessness can be mitigated.

Helplessness, PTSD, and self-efficacy

Many peoples are subjected to profoundly disrupting change that triggers anomie and learned helplessness. An important goal is to help prevent (or at least mitigate) psychological dysfunction caused by this process while encouraging positive and constructive alternatives. Ideally, social and economic "progress" will be truly beneficial and not cause pain and dysfunction.

If anomie and psychological dysfunction are analyzed with reference to trauma, PTSD, and learned helplessness, an understanding of the positive role of self-efficacy can emerge. One possible method of doing so is discussed below.

If hurtful pressures are significant enough and are not adequately addressed, significant psychological pain can develop, causing psychological dysfunction. These reactions can cause trauma in which troubled people (1) fail to acknowledge and deal with what has happened, (2) are not consciously aware of the hurtful events, and when (3) little or no mitigation takes place.

In many cases, economic and social development inflicts traumatic losses even when positive benefits simultaneously result. All too often, these negative aspects of change are not anticipated and, therefore, people are not prepared to deal with them. Under these circumstances, an analysis based on trauma and PTSD can be useful when modeling how people experience profound social and economic changes.

Harold Napoleon has specifically argued that the concept of PTSD can be used to portray how indigenous people deal with the changes wrought by the intrusion of outsiders. A broader view of trauma can usefully generalize his observations. This type of analysis can be merged with the theory of learned helplessness that demonstrates how people can become passive and fatalistic if they do not believe that they have any control over the situations they experience.

When people fail to deal with change in a proactive manner, unfortunately they can suffer and become dysfunctional. The high suicide rate often associated with anomie is one example of this potential. Thus, when fatalism is present, an inability and unwillingness to resist adverse situations can trigger counterproductive responses (or a chronic lack of response). Once this trend is set in motion, it can encourage people to accept a downward spiral.

A possible remedy under such circumstances is self-efficacy which involves people developing a belief that they have the ability to control their lives and work towards an effective response to the challenges faced. By building self-efficacy, people can gain the confidence and the resolve needed to deal with whatever

Implications of cultural trauma **87**

social changes and disruptions they face. By doing so, the tools needed to avoid dysfunction can be developed.

This model can be presented in graphic form as Table 7–6.

Trauma and PTSD often occur when people experience fear and loss. Although PTSD is often used to deal with situations involving physical danger, cultural PTSD and cultural stress can also occur, leading to hopelessness and psychological dysfunction.

Thus, cultural trauma and PTSD are akin to learned helplessness in which people come to believe that nothing they do will make any difference, leading to fatalism and apathy. Under these conditions, cultural trauma, PTSD, and anomie can lead to unmitigated sorrow and resignation, resulting in a variety of maladies, including suicide.

Self-efficacy, however, can provide people with the confidence they need to take control of their lives (instead of giving up and passively accepting what is viewed as inevitable fate). An appropriate degree of self-efficacy can mitigate anomie caused by cultural stress, hurt, and PTSD, leading to positive decisions and improved mental health.

TABLE 7–6 Beyond Trauma and PTSD

Issue	Analysis
Loss	Many indigenous, ethnic, and rural peoples face traumatic losses triggered by social and economic change.
PTSD	When changes are profound and unmitigated, responses similar to PTSD can occur.
Trauma	A generalizing of the concept of suffering that expands beyond PTSD.
Learned hopelessness	The theory of learned helplessness (that deals with people who believe they have no control over the forces they face) can be combined with the theories of trauma and PTSD to provide a more robust understanding regarding how indigenous, ethnic, and rural people respond to unmitigated change.
Fatalism	People who become fatalistic and believe they have no control over their lives can fall into a pattern of responding in passive or counterproductive ways.
Self-efficacy	Self-efficacy involves people believing that they have a degree of control over their lives. By building self-efficacy, a means of overcoming anomie, trauma, PTSD, and learned helplessness can be more effectively developed.

DISCUSSION

Anomie, PTSD, trauma, and learned helplessness can combine to convince people that they have little control over their lives. People who embrace these feelings can easily develop psychological dysfunctions. Means of strengthening the belief that people have control over their lives can lead to feelings of self-efficacy, which can help mitigate the negative implications often associated with social and economic development.

88 Psychological perspectives

Discussion questions

(1) PTSD was originally used to deal with those who faced physical danger. Do you feel it can be usefully adapted to deal with people undergoing significant change or cultural loss? Why or why not? If you believe this concept can be usefully expanded, what specific benefits does it provide?

(2) Discuss how trauma triggered by rapid and unmitigated change can be hurtful to people. Why do you think that hurtful impacts of this type are often overlooked? Why is addressing these forces important to people and those who deal with them?

(3) Discuss PTSD and the trauma of change in terms of the theory of learned helplessness. How can this response lead to people becoming passive? How can becoming passive lead to other aspects of psychological dysfunction?

(4) Envision self-efficacy as an alternative to learned helplessness. To what extent can self-efficacy counter the negative impacts of PTSD and cultural trauma?

(5) Discuss overcoming learned helplessness using self-efficacy to cope with change. Do you feel that doing so is a valuable tool to use when indigenous, ethic, and traditional people clash with the outside world? Why or why not?

References

American Psychological Association (1980). *Diagnostic and Statistical Manual of Mental Disorders.* (Washington, DC: American Psychological Association).

American Psychiatric Association (2013). *Diagnostic and Statistical Manual of Mental Disorders* (5th ed., pp. 271–280). (Arlington, VA: American Psychiatric Publishing).

Anonymous (2010, December 17). "Adverse Childhood Experiences Reported by Adults: Five States." *Weekly* 59 (49): 1609–1613.

Cash, A. (2006). *Posttraumatic Stress Disorder.* (Hoboken, NJ: Wiley).

Davis, G. (1968). *A Shoal of Time: History of the Hawaiian Islands.* (Honolulu, HI: University of Hawaii Press).

Felita, V. J., Anda, R. F. Nordenberg, D., Williamson, D., Spitz, A., Edwards, V., Koss, M., Marks, J. S. (1998). "Relationship of Childhood Abuse and Household Dysfunction to Many of the Leading Causes of Death in Adults." *American Journal of Preventive Medicine* 14 (43): 245–258.

Gilgen, M. (1996). "A Response to Harold Napoleon. . . ." In Napoleon, H. (ed.), *Yuyaruq: The Way of Being Human.* (Fairbanks, Alaska, AK: Alaska Native Knowledge Network).

HelpGuide.org. "Post-Traumatic Stress Disorder (PTSD) Symptoms, Treatment, and Self-Help for PTSD." Retrieved September 10, 2015 from found at HelpGuide.org.

Norris, F. H. & Hamblen, J. L. (2004). "Standardized Self-Report Measures of Civilian Trauma and PTSD." In Wilson, J. P., Keane, T. M. & Martin, T. (eds.), *Assessing Psychological Trauma and PTSD* (pp. 63–102). (New York: Guilford Press).

SAMHSA's Trauma and Justice Strategic Initiative (2014). *SAMHSA's Concept of Trauma and Guidance for a Trauma-Informed Approach.* (SAMHSA: United States Government).

Seligman, M. E. P. & Maier Steven, F. (1967). "Failure to Escape Traumatic Shock." *Journal of Experimental Psychology* 74 (1).

Relevant terms

ACE A model of trauma during youth. ACE stands for Adverse Childhood Experiences.

Acute PTSD Three months or less in duration.

Anxiety Disorders Section Where PTSD is discussed in *DSM* Fourth Edition.

Bandura, Albert Psychologist associated with self-efficacy.

Chronic PTSD Longer than three months in duration.

Cultural PTSD A form of PTSD caused by rapid, hurtful, and unmitigated cultural change, loss, and/or decline.

DSM The *Diagnostics and Statistical Manual* published by the American Psychological Association.

Effect A component of the 3 Es model that deals with the long-term influence of an event.

Event A component of the 3 Es model that deals with the actual event being evaluated as possibly traumatic.

Experience A component of the 3 Es model that deals with how people relate to or experience the actual event being evaluated as possibly traumatic.

Learned helplessness When animals or people have been conditioned to believe that nothing they do will have any impact on their situation and embrace passive acceptance as a result.

Life Stressor Checklist A popular assessment tool for evaluating the level of trauma. It is not designed to deal with indigenous, ethnic, and traditional people who experience cultural stress.

Napoleon, Harold Writer who identified PTSD as a contributing factor to dysfunction among Native people who experience hurtful change.

Post-traumatic stress disorder A mental disorder long associated with physical danger (or the fear of it). Can be expanded to deal with other issues, such as cultural loss.

PTSD Short for post-traumatic stress disorder.

SAMHSA Substance Abuse Mental Health Services Administration, a governmental agency concerned with mental health.

Self-efficacy The belief that people can exercise a degree of control over their lives.

Shell shock Early name for PTSD.

Soldier's heart Early name for PTSD.

Stressor Related Disorder Section Where PTSD is discussed in the Fifth Edition of the *DSM*.

Three Es model A model of trauma that emphasizes events, how people experience them, and their long-term effect.

Vietnam War Much early research on PTSD involved Vietnam veterans.

Yup'ik Alaska tribe that suffered from cultural PTSD.

8

TERROR MANAGEMENT THEORY

Learning objectives

Terror Management Theory (TMT) maintains that the fear of death can lead to suffering and dysfunction. A strong and viable cultural heritage, however, can be a powerful mitigating force by reassuring people that their heritage is immortal. When the viability of this legacy is uncertain, however, the comforting belief of cultural survival weakens, increasing the potential for psychological dysfunction. Strategies for overcoming this potential are discussed.

This chapter will:

(1) Introduce TMT and its focus upon the fear of death.
(2) Explore how psychological dysfunction can stem from the resulting anxiety.
(3) Discuss how a vital culture might mitigate the fear of death and its associated dysfunction.
(4) Analyze how dysfunction can arise if the culture is weakened or vulnerable.
(5) Consider strategies and tactics for bolstering the culture to reduce the preoccupation with death.

Introduction

The basic premise of TMT is that most people fear death and that the resulting preoccupation can exert a significant influence upon their behavior and thoughts. One means of mitigating this anxiety is for people to identify with something that is more permanent than they are. A strong social or cultural heritage can serve this alleviating role if people believe it will survive after a person dies.

As a corollary, a culture or society that is weak or in decline will probably be less able to mitigate the fear of death, leading to increased anxiety that can emerge as a catalyst for psychological dysfunction.

The case of Ishi is a powerful example of this kind of pain and suffering. Ishi was the lone survivor of a California tribe who, in the early 20th century, wandered into civilization desperate and starving. Crazed by sorrow and loneliness, he was thrown in jail. Due to his obvious Native origins, the jailors quickly called the University of California to have an anthropologist come and deal with the situation. Alfred Lewis Kroeber responded.

Ishi's story is told by Theodora Kroeber in *Ishi: The Last of his Tribe* (1964), which explores the relationship between her husband (anthropologist Alfred Louis Kroeber) and Ishi as each man comforted the other.

Theodora observes that before meeting Ishi, Kroeber had developed a severe case of depression due to the untimely death of his first wife. Confronted with Ishi, whose entire cultural universe had been destroyed, however, Kroeber came to realize that his grief over the loss of one woman was relatively insignificant when compared to the destruction of Ishi's entire world. In the process of comforting Ishi, the grieving widower was able to put his pain in perspective. Both men found salvation and inner peace by helping each other.

Once his physical and mental health returned, Ishi spent his remaining years recording and documenting his heritage, insuring its survival in some form even though it was extinct as a living society and culture. Thus, Ishi created a legacy of his culture and its people; in doing so he found the comfort that he needed to overcome his pain and the psychological dysfunctions he had initially exhibited.

Although Ishi provides an extreme example of anguish associated with cultural loss, this type of suffering and its concomitant dysfunction is often observed when cultures are weakened or destroyed or when individuals become alienated from them.

Rapid and uncontrolled social and economic change often trigger personal pain, cultural decline, and psychological dysfunction. The example of Ishi's is merely a particularly powerful and heartbreaking example.

As will be discussed, TMT can model such situations and be useful when proposing strategies for dealing with them.

Ernest Becker

In many ways, TMT is the lengthened shadow of the life and work of Ernest Becker, an anthropologist/psychologist who employed a cross-disciplinary approach and pursued eclectic techniques of teaching and conducting research. Becker's research strategies, for example, combined empirical and scientific methods of investigation alongside literary, anthropological, and humanistic insights. Because Becker's research agenda often deviated from scientific research designs that were considered to be "respectable" at the time, most psychological researchers and scholars rejected Becker and his work. Many other intellectuals, such as those in the humanities and social sciences, in contrast, found Becker's perceptions to be compelling.

Becker's key concepts are clearly stated in his book, *The Denial of Death* (1973), which won the Pulitzer Prize in 1974. Consistent with Becker's wide-ranging intellectual pedigree, this important work was inspired and influenced by, among

92 Psychological perspectives

others, Søren Kierkegaard, Sigmund Freud, and Otto Rank. Kierkegaard, of course, is a pivotal figure of existentialism, Freud emphasized the power of the unconscious, while Rank was a post-Freudian who viewed therapy as a process of learning new things and unlearning and/or discarding old and counterproductive mental habits.

The pivotal premise of *The Denial of Death* is that people fear the prospect of their own death. Becker goes on to offer the debatable assertion that people are unique in this manner because lower animals are not aware of and do not concern themselves with their eventual demise. (I personally suspect, however, that a lion that kills and eats its prey is well aware of death and its implications.)

In any event, Becker's emphasis upon death can be compared to Freud's preoccupation with sex. Freud considered sex to be the primary mainspring directing the bulk of human thought and behavior, while Becker attributed the same significance to the fear of death. Although the overarching significance of death postulated by Becker might be legitimately questioned, these fears are commonplace at both conscious and unconscious levels.

Building upon his "fear of death" hypothesis, Becker argues that human cultures and civilizations provide symbolic defense mechanisms that offer protection against the knowledge that death is inevitable. These human institutions serve both emotional and intellectual roles by providing life with meaning and by standing as a rock of permanence in a world of change and mortality. When people join with their heritage (a collectively created entity that is bigger and more pervasive than the individual), they gain a means of vicariously surviving after their own personal death. Doing so can be comforting and help relieve the recognition that life is fleeting.

Becker continues by suggesting that people join with and immerse themselves in what he calls an "immortality project" by embracing and contributing to something they consider is more permanent and eternal than they are. By believing a metaphoric part of them will never die, people reduce the sting of death. Cultures, furthermore, tend to provide people with a meaning and purpose for their lives, which is also a beneficial building block of good for mental health.

Becker, therefore, developed a theoretical foundation that suggests that an unconscious (and perhaps conscious) fear of death causes people to seek immortality by allying themselves with something that is collectively stronger and more permanent than they are individually. Doing so can help mitigate their fears.

Terror Management Theory

Thus, Becker's *The Denial of Death* is a seminal statement regarding the fear of death and the power it wields within the human psyche. Eventually, Becker's premise emerged as the primary theoretic underpinning of TMT. Aside from his pioneering contribution in writing *The Denial of Death* and other related works, Becker was unable to participate in the development of TMT because he died prematurely of cancer in 1974 while still in his forties.

In many ways, TMT can be viewed as a response and alternative to cognitive psychology which, the American Psychological Association (2013) observes, examines phenomena such as "attention, language use, memory, perception, problem solving, creativity, and thinking". Cognitive psychology has proved to be useful in a number of areas including education, economics, abnormal psychology, and so forth.

The "father" of cognitive psychology is German-born psychologist Ulric Neisser. His definitive text, *Cognitive Psychology* (1967), uses the metaphor of computers in order to describe the workings of the human mind and focus upon conscious thought. Promoted by Neisser, cognitive psychology quickly gained a loyal following. In the process, innovative strategies of conducting research were developed that dealt with subjective thought using scientific methods.

The attraction to the cognitive approach was based, in part, upon a growing dissatisfaction with behavioral psychology which for decades had limited itself to studying empirically observable behavior with little attention to the internal mental processes that underlie human actions.

Some key orientations of the cognitive approach are (1) scientific methods can model and explain human actions, (2) much behavior is the result of conscious thought, and (3) human response is triggered by various external stimuli and influences. Although cognitive psychology facilitates important lines of research, some observers have complained that depicting the human mind as a calculating device, analogous to a computer, is a gross oversimplification. As a result, more humanistic alternatives to both behaviorism and the cognitive approach have been sought.

During this era (1970s–1980s), the popularity of Ernest Becker's work was at a high point. Becker, furthermore, embraced an eclectic approach to research that often transcended the rigor of the scientific method. (For a more detailed discussion of the benefits of qualitative research see my book on the subject Walle 2015.) Here was an established psychologist (albeit eclectic, eccentric, and controversial) who possessed the humanistic and cross-disciplinary background needed to supplement and challenge behavioral and cognitive approaches to psychology.

The origins of TMT are widely known: during the 1970s, at the University of Kansas, a number of graduate students including Jeff Greenberg, Thomas Pysczn-ski, and Sheldon Solomo became interested in a broadened approach to psychology that took a lead from Becker's work.

Emerging as intellectual partners and pioneers, they adapted the basic model provided by Becker, and researched it using "respectable" methodologies because they were aware that Becker's work had been dismissed as not adequately scientific and rigorous. (This basic complaint, incidentally, has also been lodged against psychodynamic researchers and humanistic psychologists, such as Abraham Maslow.)

The result of this research agenda was the creation of TMT; a largely humanistic approach that is researched using scientific, quantitative, and "rigorous" methods. Because this research stream has appeared in a large number of peer-reviewed articles in respected scholarly journals, it cannot be dismissed on methodological

94 Psychological perspectives

grounds. As a result, TMT and its message have one foot in the humanistic camp with the other planted in "respectable" research designs. TMT and its leaders are commended for successfully walking this multi-dimensional, yet narrow, path.

Crucial to TMT, as it has evolved, is the premise that people embrace choices that mitigate the fear of death. Researchers in the field often refer to these techniques as "buffers". Two important buffers include (1) reducing "mortality salience" (the degree to which a person is preoccupied with death), and (2) developing a strong sense of self-esteem. Each is discussed.

Mortality salience

TMT uses the term mortality salience when discussing the amount of anxiety and fear that a person faces regarding their eventual death. The term "salience", of course, means something like "significance" or "importance". An individual's fear of death and its impacts can vary depending upon the situations faced, prevailing belief systems, and so forth.

Those who embrace strong religious dogmas regarding the existence of an afterlife, for example, are less vulnerable to the fear and anxiety associated with death than those who lack such comforting beliefs (Wojtkowiak and Rutjens 2011). This buffer will presumably continue to function as long as the individual's belief in life after death remains strong.

In addition, if people are exposed to something that reminds them of their own mortality, the attention to or preoccupation with death will rise and, potentially, increase the level of anxiety that is experienced.

In TMT research, the investigator typically uses some sort of manipulative technique to direct the subject's thinking towards or away from death. Having done so, the researcher measures the degree to which behavior and/or thought changes in tandem with the degree of mortality salience prompted by the specific situation.

This raises the issue regarding what factors or conditions are likely to lead to a healthy means of coping with one's mortality. Two factors that TMT acknowledges include (1) the degree of self-esteem held by the person and (2) cultural issues. These issues are related because TMT researchers emphasize that strong self-esteem is based, in part, upon an adherence to cultural standards and orientations. These buffers are discussed next.

Self-esteem as an anxiety buffer

A basic premise of TMT is that people who possess high self-esteem will experience less anxiety stemming from the fear of their eventual death. A characteristic statement of this premise (and empirical testing regarding it) is provided by Greenberg et al. (1992) and suggests that people with higher self-esteem report less anxiety when reminded of death than those possessing lower self-esteem. The implication of this observation is that people with high self-esteem are less vulnerable to fears regarding their own death. Where this is the case, people with higher esteem can be expected to suffer less psychological dysfunction triggered by this fear and anxiety.

TMT also suggests that the degree of self-esteem a person possesses is correlated with the degree to which the person adheres to their culture's codes of behavior and standards of acceptability. People who believe that they reflect their culture's ideals possess a stronger buffer against anxiety associated with death. This, in turn, can reduce dysfunction. If the culture is weakened, vulnerable, or destroyed, however, its ability to serve as a buffer can be reduced, creating a void that leading to psychological dysfunction.

The following chain of influence and action can be poised as: (1) reflecting the ideals provided by person's parents and the cultural heritage are a major building block of self-esteem; (2) when people possess higher self-esteem, they tend to be better able to mitigate the fear of death; and (3) those possessing stronger tools for mitigating the fear of death will be less vulnerable to psychological dysfunction.

The opposite situation can also be predicted. Those who do not embody these parental and cultural yardsticks of compliance tend to develop lower self-esteem and become more vulnerable to anxiety fueled by a higher degree of mortality salience. This situation can lead to higher levels of psychological dysfunction.

High self-esteem, therefore, can be a crucial building block of good mental health because it provides a buffer against disabling anxiety. Economic and social development projects, unfortunately, often disrupt local cultures and environments in ways that make it difficult or impossible for people to satisfy the demands of their culture, heritage, and traditions. This situation can undercut self-esteem. Thus, even when economic and social development projects are "beneficial", they might simultaneously reduce self-esteem among many local people, potentially leading to an epidemic of psychological dysfunction. This potential needs to be recognized and mitigated.

The role of culture

In the discussions above, reference was made to the role of culture in regulating the degree of mortality salience that people experience. That discussion indicates that although the fear of death is a powerful force, it can be mitigated by, among other things, high self-esteem. Self-esteem, in turn, tends to be influenced by cultural identity. TMT clearly recognizes this potential and its significance.

Thus, Greenberg et al. (1992, 212) observe

> culture minimizes this anxiety by providing a conception of the universe (cultural world view) that imbues the world with order, meaning, and permanence; by adhering to a set of standards of valued behavior that is satisfied, provides self-esteem; and by promising protection and, ultimately death transcendence to those who fulfill the standards of value.

96 Psychological perspectives

Earlier in this book (Chapters 2 and 6), Robert Merton's work on anomie (and its disabling psychological effects) was discussed. Although Merton was insightful, his work is concerned with cultures that function as ongoing entities that are not threatened. Under these circumstances, culture remains a strong and permanent force even though some people are unable to live up to its demands or expectations,

When discussing Merton's work, the observation was made that in many parts of the world, local cultures are vulnerable to decline and even extinction. Merton's work, unfortunately, is not designed to deal with cultures and societies that are under attack or in decline. The same basic observation can be made regarding TMT. Most TMT research concerns people who live in societies and cultures that are relatively stable (even though cultural evolution and transformation are taking place). To quote Greenberg et al. (1992, 212), the cultural models provided by TMT emphasize and suggest "permanence". Under these conditions, the level of mortality salience that people experience when they act according to cultural norms tends to be lower (i.e. not as likely to trigger psychological dysfunction). The work of Michael B Salzman is an exception to this rule.

Due to outside intrusion, such as social and economic development projects, people might come to believe that their culture, heritage, and traditions face decline and/or extinction. Under these conditions, the level of mortality salience can be expected to grow because the foundation of their lives that (1) validates their worth and justifies their self-esteem (2) proves to be fleeting and impermanent, not permanent and immortal. This recognition of cultural decline can undercut the premise that mortal individuals will live on vicariously through beloved institutions. Few TMT researchers besides Salzman, however, have considered this issue. If a subsistence hunter is denied the ability to ply his trade because compatible social and ecological environments have been ripped away, the ability to earn self-esteem will be denied. This situation has little to do with the inherent ability or worth of the individual, but reflects the loss of the venues needed to thrive, succeed, and gain respect if a culturally appropriate path is followed. Although TMT does not deny the possibility of such situations, the field has evolved within the modern, developed world and, as a result, it has seldom concentrated upon such potentials. When dealing with regions and particular peoples that are undergoing rapid, unprecedented, disruptive, and unmitigated transformations, however, this sort of loss and its ramifications are significant and need to be considered. If the culture weakens and dies, specifically, it can no longer serve as a buffer against anxiety.

Currently, some useful work in this regard is being published. Usborne and Sablonniere (2014), for example, observe that in the modern global world, ambiguity regarding a person's cultural identity is on the rise. Having stated this observation, they (2014, 436) "propose that a clear cultural identity clarifies one's personal existence, by providing a clear normative template, reducing personal uncertainty, providing an individual with a sense of continuity, and buffering an individual against the fear of death". A corollary that can be posed is that if no clear identity is present, the degree of buffering will decrease.

Thus, if the ambiguity that Usborne and Sablonniere talk about is strong enough, it potentially undercuts the lessons and directions provided by the culture, resulting in lost self-esteem capable of triggering fears, resulting in psychological dysfunction.

Most generally, such potentials are the keystone issue addressed in this book. It reflects Ernest Becker's observation that "Cultural developments might influence the fear of death" (Becker 1975, 16).

Cultural vulnerability

As indicated, many people look to their culture, traditions, and heritage as beloved extensions of their being that will live on after they are dead. Belief in this permanence offers people an opportunity to envision a vicarious survival after their physical death. When the anxieties regarding death are reduced in this manner, the psychological dysfunction exhibited by people and their communities can be reduced. This mitigation, however, is hinged around people believing that their culture, traditions, and heritage are strong and will continue to survive indefinitely.

Where economic, technological, and social change are rapidly undercutting local cultures and traditions, this might not be the case. When people believe their heritage is dying, they often experience psychological dysfunction because the cloak of emotional support provided by a person's way of life no longer provides comfort.

Michael Salzman (2001) provides pioneering work that connects terror management with dysfunction among indigenous people experiencing profound change and loss due to the intrusion of outsiders and their influence. In particular, Salzman's analysis has shown how TMT can usefully model how people respond not only to physical death, but to the destruction of their culture and heritage. Although these connections can be (and have been) made by researchers such as Salzman, the bulk of TMT research has proceeded in other directions, presumably because of the interests and concerns of the investigators. Salzman, however, demonstrates that TMT is rich and robust enough to deal with small and threatened cultural enclaves facing significant challenges.

Walle (2004), whose work was discussed earlier in this book, has developed a model similar to Salzman's when dealing with the dysfunction exhibited by the Iroquois Indians in the late 18th to early 19th centuries. TMT, therefore, provides a means of dealing with distinctive ethnic groups facing stress and loss due to the disruptive pressures.

Salzman (2001); Salzman and Halloran (2004), and Salzman (2005), furthermore, have dealt with the relationship between culture, self-esteem, and anxiety that was triggered by powerful outside forces that intrude into the lives of indigenous people. Using TMT, they argue that when a culture faces great trauma, self-esteem will be lowered and become a less effective buffer against the fear of death. Feelings of inferiority, furthermore, can easily develop.

98 Psychological perspectives

In short, if people believe their culture is a strong force that will survive after they die, it can serve as a buffer against mortality salience in ways that can reduce psychological dysfunction. If, in contrast, people conclude that their culture, heritage, and traditions are weakening or dying, this heritage tends to provide less comfort and salience. In many parts of the world, cultures and societies are experiencing profound transitions. In these environments, declining and shattered cultures can no longer serve as viable buffers against anxiety. Just the opposite: the elimination of traditions and heritage can emerge as an additional source of grief and depression. This combination of stress and anxiety can lead to increased psychological dysfunction. Such trends are often observed and reported.

Comparing TMT with the theory of anomie

Earlier in this chapter, we discussed TMT with reference to the theory of anomie as it was developed by Robert Merton. That discussion demonstrates parallels between Merton's work and TMT because both tend to focus upon cultures that were "going concerns". As we saw above, however, this is not always the case; under many circumstances, cultures are weakened, fragile, or in decline.

Earlier chapters of this book discussed anomie, as originally developed by Emile Durkheim, and how it dealt with the hurtful impacts of social change and cultural decline upon distinctive people (typically rural, ethnic enclaves). Durkheim's pioneering work focused upon a breakdown in the collective values, morals, and expectations of small social and cultural groups, observing that when the level of anomie is high, psychological dysfunction (such as suicide) increases. Although Merton deals with homogeneous cultures, not isolated groups as Durkheim does, he expands Durkheim's thinking by discussing specific ways in which people respond to alienating pressures. (Applications of Merton's model are discussed in Chapter 6.) Some of the responses parallel TMT's observations regarding high degrees of mortality salience. In other situations, Merton demonstrates how people might devise effective strategies for coping with the situation in a more productive manner.

As discussed in Chapter 2, Merton stated that the cause of anomie was the inability to achieve culturally accepted standards in socially acceptable ways. When such situations occur, people can either (1) adjust to evolving circumstances or (2) bear the brunt of failure that is likely to trigger a loss of self-esteem. When this occurs, dysfunction is a likely result.

A comparison of these TMT and the theory of anomie is presented in Table 8–1.

Notice the parallels and similarities between these two independent research streams. Parallels of this type are often used as an indication of accuracy by qualitative investigators. The research method used to do so is usually called "triangulation".

Triangulation (Walle 2015, 145), simply put, "refers to the process of examining a phenomenon in more than one way in order to provide a more robust analysis".

TABLE 8–1 Terror Management Theory and Anomie Compared

Issue	Terror management	Anomie
Type of theory	A psychological theory that deals with the fear of death and its impacts.	A sociological theory that deals anxiety caused by stressful situations.
Cultural conformity	Those who conform to the norms of their culture reduce their fear of death.	Those who achieve cultural goals in acceptable ways are less impacted by anomie.
Threats	The inability to conform can lead to an increased fear of death.	Those who cannot achieve cultural goals in acceptable ways suffer from anomie.
Mental health	Those with higher self-esteem exhibit fewer psychological problems due to a fear of death and so forth.	Those who achieve cultural goals in acceptable ways experience lower levels of hurtful deviant behavior.
Dysfunction	People with lower self-esteem possess increased psychological dysfunction (fear of death and its impacts).	The anomie and alienation triggered by rapid and unmitigated social change can lead to dysfunction, including suicide.

DISCUSSION

Although these theories stem from different intellectual traditions (psychology and social science), they are clearly parallel because each is concerned with the significance of (1) people conforming to cultural standards and (2) the degree of mental health vs. dysfunction that derives from doing (or not doing) so. These two theories can be used in conjunction with each other or even merged.

In the mid-1960s, Webb et al. (1966) noted that "once a proposition has been confirmed by two or more independent measurement processes . . . uncertainty . . . is greatly reduced". Denzin (1970) expanded the value of the technique by pointing to a variety of ways in which it can be practiced including: (1) data triangulation (gathering a variety of data), (2) investigator triangulation (using more than one investigator), (3) theoretical triangulation (interpreting the data using more than one theory), and (4) methodological triangulation (gathering and analyzing data using more than one method).

When comparing the research of TMT investigators and anomie-oriented sociologists, important similarities arise that emerge as a de facto application of triangulation. First, different data sets are used. Second, the investigators are different. Third, psychology and sociology are different disciplines with distinct theoretic orientations. And fourth, the methods of conducting research are diverse. Even with these significant and multiple differences, clear parallels exist in their respective findings.

100 Psychological perspectives

Bolstered by these parallels and the credibility they provide, the following chain of thought can be suggested:

(1) A high degree of mortality salience leads to a growing fear of death that can trigger psychological dysfunction.
(2) High self-esteem can mitigate or buffer the fear of death and, thereby, lessen dysfunction.
(3) A vital culture can be viewed as an immortal force that will continue after individual members die and provide a means of vicariously surviving after death. Doing so can reduce the fear of death and concomitant dysfunctional behavior. This is parallel to a culture/people that are not suffering from anomie.
(4) Conversely, weak, declining, and vulnerable cultures will be less able to serve this role. The eclipse of the culture, furthermore, will render the yardsticks of evaluation that people use to build and maintain self-esteem passé. Under these conditions, self-esteem can be expected to decline, leading to an increase in psychological dysfunction. Anomie will also be more of a problem.

These conclusions usefully combine the work of TMT and anomie into a more complex and robust model.

Strategies and tactics

TMT, therefore, poses a relationship between psychological dysfunction and the fear of death. Strong cultures, however, can serve as a mitigating force that counters these anxieties. If mortality salience is reduced in this way, people can be expected to exhibit less and/or milder episodes of psychological dysfunction.

A number of strategies can be proposed that, consistent with this approach, might reduce psychological dysfunction among people who experience significant economic and social change. These options include (1) preserving the heritage, (2) replacing the heritage, and (3) fostering an orderly transition. Each is briefly discussed.

> **Preserve heritage**: Many peoples (and their advocates) seek to preserve the local heritage, including maintaining traditional ways of life, preserving the indigenous languages, and so forth. This strategy can create continuity between the past and the future, and might help to reduce tensions among different generations who are still living. Although paying homage to the past has benefits, under some circumstances, doing so might inhibit people from responding to changing conditions in a productive and beneficial manner. If so, preserving local traditions might inadvertently make the culture less competitive and less able to positively adjust to changing conditions. In addition, some members of the younger generation who (1) connect with the modern, outside world and (2) might not respond well to the past might not relate well to this strategy.

Replace heritage: One of the classic strategies employed by dominant outside forces that seek to influence distinctive peoples involves encouraging (or even forcing) them to reject their old ways of life and embrace the mainstream world. In the United States and elsewhere, for example, young indigenous people were ripped from their communities and required to spend their formative years in boarding schools far from home. The overt goal of doing so was to reprogram the minds of future indigenous leaders so they would reject their traditional heritage and embrace mainstream ways. Such aggressive tactics, unfortunately, often lead to profound psychological dysfunction among many former boarding school students, including a high rate of alcoholism. This alarming level of dysfunction appears to result from profound alienation that arises when students develop in ways that make them unable to "fit" into either their culture or the mainstream world. These displaced individuals suffered as a result. Local communities, furthermore, often face chaos as internal struggles and misunderstanding grow. Today, strategies aiming at forcibly undercutting the local culture are not as prevalent as they once were and they tend to be heavily criticized (and, in the author's opinion, rightfully so).

Even though governmental policies might no longer emphasize this method, economic conditions and initiatives often continue to function in a parallel manner. Thus, economic development, job prospects, and other opportunities potentially pull people away from their heritage and, thereby, eliminate the comfort and security it once provided. Under such circumstances, psychological dysfunction can be expected to rise.

Orderly transition: Other strategies acknowledge that change is inevitable while simultaneously taking active steps to involve local people and the community in the decision-making process. Initiatives such as these typically seek to help people embrace change on their own terms and with a clear understanding of the tradeoffs involved. Strategies can be developed that strive to preserve and nurture vital aspects of the culture while simultaneously accepting some a degree of inevitable change. Following such an approach, tactics that reduce the tendencies for cultural disruption can be employed as transitions are phased in. In this way, people who follow the old ways can be given respect, honor, and protection from the anxiety associated with unmitigated change. By doing so, anomie and the degree of mortality salience can be reduced and, hopefully, the level of psychological dysfunction will be lower.

These strategies can be juxtaposed in Table 8–2.

Thus, a variety of approaches exist for indigenous, ethnic, and traditional peoples to employ as increased contact with the outside world takes place. Different strategies embrace different levels of risk regarding anomie and high levels of mortality salience. When social and economic development take place, these risks need to be determined and, where necessary, mitigated.

102 Psychological perspectives

TABLE 8–2 Strategies Compared

Strategy	Description	Analysis
Preserve heritage	Mortality salience might be reduced at least in the short term, but positive adjustment to new conditions might be inhibited. Those who do not identify with traditions might be alienated.	This strategy often has a high profile as efforts are made to preserve cultures and languages. Reviving traditional arts and activities can have positive results. But will such initiatives be sustainable?
Replace heritage	Dominant outsiders often urge distinctive people to assimilate. Coercive tactics are often used to insure compliance.	Forced assimilation has largely been replaced with economic strategies that undermine traditions causing mortality salience and psychological dysfunction to increase.
Orderly transition	The outside world is powerful and often cannot be avoided. Choosing appropriate adjustment strategies can be empowering and reduce mortality salience and dysfunction.	If informed people make thoughtful decisions, positive and empowering strategies can result even if a potential for failure exists (that might trigger devastating cultural, economic, and psychological disruption).

DISCUSSION

People experiencing profound change need strategies that minimize social and psychological stress. Otherwise, high levels of mortality salience and anomie are likely to increase psychological dysfunction.

Discussion

Terror Management Theory is a school of psychology that deals with the fear of death and its power over people. When this anxiety is not adequately "buffered" (or mitigated), it is likely to trigger psychological dysfunction within specific people. The sociological theory of anomie provides a similar assessment.

Combined, TMT and anomie can be used to deal with the anxiety caused by rapid and unmitigated change and how to counter these hurtful pressures. Specific insights and components of this work include:

(1) Cultural loss can eliminate important coping mechanisms, resulting in increased fears, pain, and anxiety.
(2) Higher levels of fear, pain, and anxiety can be a catalyst for social and psychological dysfunction.
(3) One method of buffering/mitigating these hurtful feelings (and the dysfunction that stems from them) is for people to envision cultures as immortal and continuing after people die. If people believe their culture will survive, the fear of death can be mitigated.

Terror Management Theory **103**

(4) Another option is to help people to more effectively cope with profound change so they can manage their losses and/or replace them with positive options in ways that reduce anxiety.
(5) These two strategies can work in tandem with each other.
(6) In both cases, techniques that seek to reduce psychological pain and dysfunction are introduced.

Although more work needs to be accomplished if this strategy is to reach its full potential, this chapter discusses TMT as a method capable of serving the needs of indigenous, ethnic, and traditional people experiencing change. This approach has much to offer; I expect the future will see additional developments in this area.

Discussion questions

(1) Ernest Becker inspired TMT by proposing a specific theory regarding human behavior that involved the fear of death. To what extent can this theory be useful when dealing with changing conditions faced by cultural enclaves? Give an example.
(2) TMT explores how psychological dysfunction often results from the fear of death. How can cultural decline or weakness keep the culture from serving as a buffer that mitigates the fear of death? Discuss relevant implications of this possibility. Give an example.
(3) Discuss how a vital culture might mitigate the fear of death and reduce the dysfunction associated with personal morality. How can a knowledge of such possibilities be useful when devising ways for communities to participate in economic and social development initiatives?
(4) How can the process of planning and strategic development benefit from the concepts provided by TMT? How might the application of these insights prevent future dysfunction? What are some problems that can be reduced or mitigated by doing so? Give an example.
(5) Using an example of your own choosing, consider strategies and tactics for reducing psychological dysfunction by strengthening the culture in order to reduce mortality salience.

References

American Psychological Association (2013). *Glossary of Psychological Terms*. Retrieved June 13, 2015 from Apa.org.
Becker, E. (1973). *The Denial of Death*. (New York: Simon & Schuster).
Becker, E. (1975). *Escape from Evil*. (New York: Free Press).
Denzin, N. K. (1970). *The Research Act in Sociology*. (Chicago, IL: Aldine).
Greenberg, J., Pyscznski, T., Solomon, S. & Chatel, D. (1992). "Terror Management Tolerance: Does Mortality Salience Always Intensify Negative Reactions to Others Who Threaten One's Worldview?" *Journal of Personality and Social Psychology* 63: 212–220.
Kroeber, T. (1964). *Ishi: The Last of His Tribe*. (Berkley, CA: University of California Press).

104 Psychological perspectives

Neisser, U. (1967). *Cognitive Psychology.* (Englewood Cliffs, NJ: Prentice-Hall).

Salzman, M. B. (2001). "Cultural Trauma and Recovery: Perspectives from Terror Management Theory." *Trauma, Violence, and Abuse* 2 (2): 172–191.

Salzman, M. B. (2005). "The Dynamics of Cultural Trauma: Implications for the Pacific Nations." In: Marsella, A. J., Austin, A. & Grant, B. (eds.), *Social Change and Psychosocial Adaptation in the Pacific Islands: Cultures in Transition* (pp. 29–52). (New York: Springer).

Salzman, M. B. & Halloran, M. J. (2004). "Cultural Trauma and Recovery: Cultural Meaning, Self-Esteem, and the Re-Construction of the Cultural Anxiety-Buffer." In Greenberg, J., Koole, S. L. & Pyszczynski, T. (eds.), *Handbook of Experimental Existential Psychology* (pp. 231–246). (New York: Guilford).

Usborne, E. & Sablonniere, R. (2014). "Understanding My Culture Means Understanding Myself: The Function of Cultural Identity Clarity for Personal Identity Clarity and Personal Psychological Well-Being." *Journal for the Theory of Social Behaviour* 44 (4): 436–458.

Walle, Alf H. (2004). *The Path of Handsome Lake: A Model of Recovery for Native People.* (Charlotte, NC: Information Age Publishers).

Walle, Alf H. (2015). *Qualitative Research in Business: A Practical Overview.* (Newcastle, UK: Cambridge Scholars).

Webb, E. J., Campbell, D. T., Schwartz, R. D. & Sechrest, L. (1966). *Unobtrusive Measures: Nonreactive Measures in the Social Sciences.* (Chicago, IL: Rand McNally).

Wojtkowiak, J. & Rutjens, B. T. (2011). "The Postself and Terror Management Theory: Reflecting on after Death Identity Buffers Existential Threat." *The International Journal for the Psychology of Religion* 21 (2): 137–144.

Relevant terms

Becker, Ernest   Psychologist/anthropologist who inspired Terror Management Theory.

Buffers   Phenomena that temper and/or reduce the fear of death.

Cognitive Psychology   A branch of psychology arising in the 1970s that focuses upon conscious and purposeful thought.

Cultural vulnerability   A culture or society being weak or declining in ways that prevent it from adequately buffering the fear of death.

Culture   According to TMT, a strong culture can be a powerful buffer against the fear of death. A weaker culture might lack that ability.

Denial of death   According to TMT, a denial of death is a common preoccupation of people.

Freud, Sigmund   A psychiatrist who influenced Ernest Becker.

Greenberg, Jeff   A leader of TMT.

Immortality project   Efforts that people exert in order for something they create to live on after they die, providing vicarious immortality.

Ishi   An indigenous man of California who emerged as the last member of his tribe and suffered as a result.

Kierkegaard, Søren   A pioneer of existentialism who influenced Ernest Becker.

Maslow, Abraham   Important humanistic psychologist.

Mortality salience   The degree to which the fear of death is a pressing concern for the individual. This can vary over time and due to conditions. Low mortality salience is a buffer against the fear of death.

Neisser, Ulric   A leader of cognitive psychology.

Pyscznski, Thomas   A leader of TMT.

Terror Management Theory **105**

Rank, Otto Important psychiatrist and therapist who influenced Ernest Becker.

Self-esteem According to TMT, high self-esteem is a buffer against the fear of death.

Solomon, Sheldon A leader of TMT.

Terror Management Theory (TMT) A theory of psychology that focuses upon the impact of the fear of death upon people.

EPILOGUE TO SECTION 2

Disruptive change, often involving social or economic development, can lead to a wide variety of stresses, vulnerabilities, needs, and dysfunctions. On many unfortunate occasions, these hurtful implications are not adequately anticipated and addressed.

When difficulties surface or potentially arise, techniques for analysis, prevention and mitigation are needed. A variety of techniques exist in this regard. Section 2 discusses a representative sample of these methods. Due to limits of space, this discussion does not claim to be exhaustive. The goal is merely to point to a range of options that exists as well as the continuity to be found within that diversity.

The concept of anomie is a keystone of this book. It deals with change and how it can lead to stress and psychological dysfunction. Due to the importance of the concept of anomie, Section 2 begins with an expanded discussion of anomie as well as the analysis of a variety of ways in which specific people respond to and are affected by it. This includes both positive and negative alternatives. Robert Merton's typology of reactions to anomie is especially useful, particularly after it has been adjusted to deal with communities and social groups that are distinct from powerful intruding forces and/or from mainstream society.

Additional theories and methods were also discussed in order to emphasize the fact that unanticipated and uncontrolled change can take a profound toll upon people who are not prepared to cope with it. In this regard, Chapter 7 expanded the discussion by dealing with feelings of loss, fear, and change with reference to PTSD. Chapter 8 examined TMT and its focus upon the fear of death. Both of these theories were adjusted to deal with cultural issues.

TMT, building upon the work of Ernest Becker, suggests that the fear of death is a major (if not the dominant) force impacting society and human behavior. A strong culture, however, can serve as a buffer or mitigating force that counteracts this fear and tempers dysfunctional reactions to it. A weakened or vulnerable culture, however, can no longer serve this vital role; thus, an enfeebled heritage can fuel psychological dysfunction. Strengthening and rebuilding the culture, in contrast, can lead to better psychological health because doing so can help people believe that a part of them will vicariously live on in the institutions they love.

Section 2, therefore, discussed specific examples of how social and economic change can lead to psychological dysfunction among indigenous, ethnic, and traditional people. These chapters set the stage to consider particular techniques for preventing and/or mitigating these hurtful influences.

Building upon this work, Section 3 offers more detailed suggestions regarding the prevention and mitigation of psychological dysfunction potentially caused by social and economic change. These suggestions will, hopefully, be useful to a wide array of practitioners, including business strategists, social planners, social workers, and psychological therapists.

SECTION 3
Strategies of mitigation

PROLOGUE TO SECTION 3

Section 2 provided useful orientations for understanding how social and economic change can encourage psychological dysfunction among indigenous, ethnic, and traditional people. Due to the distinctiveness of such populations, specific (not generic) techniques are needed for dealing with and mitigating these hurtful forces. Section 3 explores this reality in tailored and practitioner-oriented ways.

Chapter 9, "Client-centered therapy", begins with a comparison of Cultural Safety and Cultural Competence, two initiatives that seek to insure that counselors, therapists, and other health care providers adequately focus upon the beliefs, fears, hopes, goals, and so forth of those being served. After taking the distinctiveness of clients into account, models of therapy and recovery that recognize their traditions and heritage are considered. Doing so begins with a discussion of the ubiquitous Stages of Change model that can be used to calculate what people actually want and if they are willing to change. Providing a typology ranging from a lack of interest in new options to taking action to achieve them, the counselor is reminded that not all people possess the same goals and levels of dedication to a particular course of action.

Having considered these feelings, the counselor or therapist is offered perspectives that reflect and focus upon the those being served. Doing so can be enhanced by the work of Carl Rogers and his "client-centered" style of treatment. Currently, however, more streamlined and focused treatment plans are commonly employed. This trend has led to the establishment of "semi-directed" methods such as Motivational Interviewing that can help therapists and counselors concentrate treatment in some ways while simultaneously doing so in ways that reflect the needs and desires of indigenous, ethnic, and traditional people.

Building upon this background, Chapter 10, "Representative tactics", briefly analyzes two specific methods of intervention that can be adapted for use with

112 Strategies of mitigation

indigenous, ethnic, and traditional peoples. These techniques, of course, are representative and not exhaustive.

In particular, (1) Gregory Bateson's combining cybernetics (information theory) with anthropology and (2) René Girard's work with role-modeling and its implications are adapted for use with those experiencing change and anomie.

Bateson was concerned with the impacts of a reshuffling of power and authority and the stress that results. When people lose power, others tend to fill the void. Once in a position of authority, many people hesitate to relinquish the clout they have gained. As a result, problems can develop if rehabilitated people seek to regain their decision-making status. Although Bateson dealt primarily with alcoholics, a modified version of this model can focus upon social and/or economic changes, the powershifts associated with it, as well as the resulting psychological impacts.

René Girard, whose work parallels Bateson in some ways, suggests that much of the world's pain and conflict is caused by a tendency to imitate others in hurtful ways (which he refers to as "mimesis"). When people emulate others, they develop similar interests and desires. This can lead to envy, rivalry, and tensions due to the competition that emerges. Social and psychological dysfunction can result. Girard's model can be useful when analyzing responses that can occur when social and economic change impinges upon people and their desires.

By adapting the work of observers such as Bateson and Girard, methods for dealing with anomie, culture loss, and alienation can be developed.

The two examples outlined in Chapter 10 are representative and not exhaustive. Many other tools can be adjusted to serve indigenous, ethnic, and traditional people. It is hoped that these examples will help others envision how to adjust their toolkit to more effectively deal with the circumstances they face.

9

CLIENT-CENTERED THERAPY

Learning objectives

Recognizing the distinctiveness of specific people is an important aspect of therapy. The methods of Cultural Safety and Cultural Competence are two ways of doing so. In addition, understanding how clients relate to therapy is important. Client-centered therapy involves allowing clients to help formulate the issues that will be dealt with in therapy. Today, however, client-centered strategies are being replaced with semi-directed techniques that involve both clients and therapists in the decision-making process. Issues addressed include:

(1) The value of Cultural Safety and Cultural Competence within therapy.
(2) Adapting the Stages of Change model to depict people as they are.
(3) Grasping the value of Carl Rogers' client-centered methods.
(4) Understanding how Motivational Interviewing can provide direction to client-centered therapy.
(5) Recognizing the value of accepting people on their own terms.

Introduction

One strategy for helping people overcome psychological problems is for the provider of help and services to emerge as an authority figure, role model, and/or a dominant force who sets agendas and tactics. Although some people might benefit from this sort of authoritative arrangement, it is not inherently empowering, and can fail to meet people on their own terms.

This observation has implications both for professional counselors and therapists and for lay people who are involved with self-help organizations such as Alcoholics Anonymous (I am a state-certified substance abuse therapist and have

114 Strategies of mitigation

practitioner experience in the field). AA members, for example, often make observations such as "Your best thinking got you here" in order (1) to emphasize that newcomers should do what they are told and (2) to assert that those with experience in the program have the answers. For better or worse, many interventions (both self-help and professional) ultimately develop into overt or covert power relationships or struggles.

The logic underlying such tactics is that novices who passively accept what is offered and follow instructions in lock-step fashion have a better chance of effectively dealing with their problems. Others, who follow their own path, are often predicted to continue suffering (or in the words of *The Big Book* of Alcoholics Anonymous, "their chances are less than average").

The tone of such therapy and self-help, of course, is similar to the dictates of many economic development and/or social change specialists who believe that they possess tools of universal application that everyone (including indigenous, ethnic, and traditional peoples) should embrace. On many occasions, however, the methods introduced by outsiders do not achieve their desired goals. Worse yet, hurtful and unanticipated side effects might emerge. Such unintended consequences are especially likely if those providing help lack culturally sensitivity. The opposite alternative is for therapists to listen carefully to what their clients say and help them craft programs that fit who they are and what they want. Doing so involves abandoning the "top-down" belief that the therapist (or economic consultant) invariably possesses superior and applicable insights. Thus, a "bottom-up" approach (which embraces more of a client orientation) might be more effective in tailoring interventions so they help people in a uniquely appropriate manner. This approach (adjusting, preserving, and responding to clients in tailored ways) can be an excellent strategy. In order to help clients and peoples to achieve this sort of empowerment, those who help others need to understand those they serve. Two techniques for doing so are known as Cultural Safety and Cultural Competence. Having compared these two approaches, a number of client-sensitive therapeutic approaches are discussed that address the needs of distinctive peoples on their own terms. These tools include the Stages of Growth model, the work of Carl Rogers, and Motivational Interviewing (MI). These tools are representative of techniques that can combat the power of anomie in a culturally sensitive and appropriate manner.

Cultural Safety

The Cultural Safety movement is a significant attempt to offer health care in ways that are nurturing and relevant to members of specific communities (such as indigenous peoples, ethnic minorities, and traditional enclaves) and their heritages. It was initially associated with members of the nursing profession in New Zealand who served the Maori people, a large indigenous minority in that country (Wepa 2015). Best viewed within the larger context of Maori culture and society and the struggle for equity and parity within New Zealand, the movement seeks to insure that Maori clients and patients will receive culturally appropriate treatment, ideally from fellow Maori.

Key aspects of the Cultural Safety initiative include four principles (National Council For Nursing in New Zealand 2005, 4–6) that, in part, charge health care practitioners with: (1) recognizing the beliefs and practices of those they serve, (2) acknowledging power relationships, empowering clients, adopting social scientific perspectives, and so on, (3) identifying inequalities, especially those created by history, politics, and so on, and (4) recognizing that health care potentially acts as a barrier that prevents people from embracing positive aspects of their heritage.

Policies and strategies embracing such principles, of course, can go a long way towards relieving the suffering caused by inappropriate, ineffective, and inefficient care. It is praised for that reason. It must also be noted that the Cultural Safety movement is a product of a large ethnic group, the Maori of New Zealand. This demographic reality creates the "critical mass" allowing programs, policies, and strategies to be developed that are directly and uniquely aimed at this group.

To its credit, furthermore, the Maori have many highly educated people. When we were both at the University of Alaska at Fairbanks, for example, I got to know Graham Smith, a noted New Zealand educator of Maori descent who initiated a plan to insure a large number of Maori would be able to receive doctoral (and other advanced) degrees within a short period of time. It is my understanding that Smith was successful in his quest to do so. Thus, the Maori are very different from many indigenous peoples that are small in number with few members having a "formal education".

Although, the Cultural Safety movement has at times been characterized as polemical and overly centered around the Maori and its history, Gerlach (2012) observes "there is emerging evidence of its capacity to promote a more critical discourse on culture, health, and health care inequities and how they are shaped by historical, political, and socio–economic circumstances".

Cultural Safety, therefore, has emerged as a means of tailoring appropriate health care in ways that more effectively serve a particular people in ways that, hopefully, temper biases, vested interests, and misunderstandings that can arise if outsiders dominate. In many parts of the world, the spirit of such initiatives has a significant contribution to make. Table 9–1 outlines key aspects of Cultural Safety.

Cultural Safety, therefore, has the potential to emerge as a major tool of significant relevance to indigenous people, ethnic groups, and traditional enclaves. It was, however, developed within the political context of New Zealand and has largely focused on a specific indigenous group, the Maori. Not only can this make specific applications partisan and polemical, it is centered around a large indigenous population with a significant educated cohort. These aspects appear to limit its universality. Nevertheless, attempts are being made to expand the range of the Cultural Safety movement by, for example, dealing with the needs of Muslim immigrants (Baker 2007) and Canadian First Nations peoples (Aboriginal Nurses Association of Canada, Canadian Association of Schools of Nursing (CASN), and Canadian Nurses Association 2009).

116 Strategies of mitigation

TABLE 9-1 Cultural Safety: An Overview

Issue	Description	Analysis
Need	Outsiders are apt to employ "culturally loaded" perspectives. Community members intuitively possess insights of therapeutic value.	Outsiders may be culturally blind and/or harbor views that inhibit their ability to serve specific clients. Local practitioners can mitigate this problem.
Cultural distinctiveness	Specific cultures possess structures and patterns that are easily overlooked by outsiders but recognized by local practitioners.	Outsiders tend to offer "generic" and universal tools and methods. Local practitioners can add valuable culturally specific orientations.
Distinctive dysfunctions	Because of cultural and historic differences, specific people often suffer in specific and distinct ways.	Members of a culture or community possess an insider's knowledge that can be of value to therapy.
Benefits	Practitioners from the community can more intuitively understand clients and serve them in appropriate ways.	More suitable tools of therapy and intervention can be developed by members of the community.

DISCUSSION

Cultural Safety seeks to temper the limitations of outside professionals by providing more locally based therapy. Because outsiders may lack an adequate cultural grounding, local practitioners have a vital role to play.

Cultural Competence

When people work with well-trained and experienced practitioners who possess a similar cultural background, they can avoid dealing with outsiders or those who are likely to possess cultural gaps that cause them to be ineffective. Unfortunately, on many occasions, few local people possess the training and skills that are required.

This reality has resulted in an emphasis upon Cultural Competence that, in a nutshell, seeks to provide practitioners with the degree of cultural understanding they need to be effective. Thus, if local people are not available as practitioners, those who are available will be provided with the cultural training and insights needed to be effective.

Although this is a noble cause, in recent years concerns have arisen regarding the Cultural Competence movement (or at least the way it is dealt with in graduate seminars on the topic). These criticisms, however, tend to result from specific applications, not with the essence of the concept. In that regard Kirmayer (2012) has observed that Cultural Competence is sometimes criticized because it often narrowly includes only five large groups: Afro Americans, Asian Americans, Pacific Islanders, Latinos, American Indians/Alaska Natives, and White. Certainly the cultural makeup of the United States (and the world) is larger than this and the full range of variation needs to be addressed and recognized.

Although some cultural groups (such as those listed by Kirmayer and others such as the Maori) are large in number, many cultural groups are small and have few formally trained practitioners. In addition, from a demographic perspective, therapists and counselors tend to skew towards specific cultural and ethnic backgrounds. Although this situation is lamentable and needs to be rectified, it currently exists in many places. In this environment, developing Cultural Competence must be relied upon to help practitioners develop an adequate degree of cultural awareness and empathy.

Raised in East Tennessee (USA) many years ago, I was a member of my high school football team. During one season, the grandfather of a teammate died. The man's last wish was that the entire team would be his pallbearers. We obliged, showing up at a small, rural house of worship in our black and gold football jerseys to honor the request. Once inside, I saw people mumbling to themselves in an incoherent manner. Others were lying on the ground, rolling around and shaking. Coming from a rather sheltered background, I was frightened and convinced that these people had lost their minds.

But they had not. The members of this church were merely practicing a religious tradition known as "speaking in tongues". Far from being psychologically dysfunctional, they were merely worshiping in a distinctive manner that is very different from mainstream religion. Due to my love of old-time gospel music, I eventually began visiting churches where people spoke in tongues; in the process of doing so, I came to accept such behavior as a natural thing. That first experience, however, had been quite unnerving.

Imagine psychiatrists, therapists, or social workers who had been raised and trained in a typical mainstream environment with no knowledge of or exposure with those who speak in tongues. How do you think these mental health practitioners would view people who acted in such a manner? Such mainstream professionals could easily conclude that the people they saw were experiencing profound psychological problems. This assessment, however, would be wrong.

The term Cultural Competence reminds us that those who provide help need to pursue their profession with reference to the cultural context in which they work and with a sensitivity towards the traditions and heritage of their clients. In other words, therapists should not confuse cultural distinctiveness with psychological dysfunction. Developing culturally competent skills and perspectives is especially important when practitioners work with distinctive people who differ significantly from their own background.

An interest in Cultural Competence can be traced back to the late 1980s and the work of Terry Cross and his colleagues. The seminal publication in the field, *Towards a Culturally Competent System of Care*, was published in 1989. By the turn of the century, significant attention was being directed towards specific cultural

118 Strategies of mitigation

issues, not merely universal strategies of health care. In 2002, the United States Department of Minority Health published *Teaching Cultural Competence in Health Care: A Review of Current Concepts, Policies and Practices*. Today, Cultural Competence has emerged as a distinct and respected subfield in the health care industry; scholars, teachers, and practitioners are increasingly exposed to its principles. For a discussion of progress in the field, consult (Thackrah and Thompson 2013). An overview of Cultural Competence is presented in Table 9–2.

The Cultural Competence movement reminds therapists to focus upon their clients' heritage and point of view. By doing so, clients can be more effectively served. Although such thinking has emerged as a truism, in actual practice not all professionals have mastered these skills.

Thus, Cultural Safety and Cultural Competence are two related, but distinct, techniques for insuring that health care professionals possess a sophisticated and appropriate cultural understanding. Cultural Safety arose to serve a large indigenous group (the Maori) that sought greater control over the therapy and care its members receive. Cultural Competence, in contrast, was designed to help alien

TABLE 9–2 Cultural Competence: An Overview

Issue	Description	Analysis
Need	People are more than generic creatures. They are molded by their culture and heritage. Therapists need to be aware of this fact.	The behavior and responses of people are the result of two influences: their innate humanity and the specifics of their culture.
Cultural distinctiveness	Cultures harbor specific beliefs regarding, life, death, the purpose of existence, and so forth. These components exert profound influences.	Although cultures are significant, the power they have upon both therapists and clients is often overlooked. These influences need to be recognized and addressed.
Psychological dysfunction	Cultural traits can make people vulnerable to specific stresses and tensions that trigger dysfunction. These potentials need to be acknowledged.	By understanding the client's culture and heritage, therapists can more effectively perceive the pressures facing the client and envision strategies of effective therapy.
Benefits	Cultural Competence can help therapists deal with people on their own terms and in appropriate ways.	More effective tools of therapy and intervention can be developed if clients and their way of life are understood.

DISCUSSION

Cultural Competence is increasingly recognized as an invaluable tool that can help replace and temper overly generic tools of intervention. Because rapid cultural change can cause dysfunction, envisioning these tensions from a culturally competent perspective is vital.

practitioners develop the cultural empathy and understanding needed to serve culturally distinctive clients. Both initiatives are praised.

Having pointed to the growing emphasis upon cultural sensitivity, a range of specific tools are discussed that deal with psychological stress and dysfunction in ways that avoid ethnocentrism. Such culturally aware approaches are of particular value when dealing with indigenous, ethnic, and traditional people who are exposed to significant change.

Stages of Change model

One of the most popular techniques of contemporary therapy is the Stages of Change approach, more formally known as the Transtheoretical Model. This technique was first developed by James Prochaska and his co-workers in the 1970s. Over the years, it has gained popularity among therapists who help those with bad habits (such as smoking) or addictions (including alcoholism) and, increasingly, in other situations. Useful overviews of the Stages of Change method are available including Prochaska and Velicer (1997) and Prochaska et al. (1994).

In essence, the Stages of Change approach suggests that people proceed through a number of steps as their thinking and behavior is transformed in positive ways. The process is viewed as a continuum involving particular opinions, motivations, degrees of dedication to a goal, and so forth. This formulation has almost emerged as an article of faith within the therapeutic community and among laypeople.

The first stage is "precontemplation": a period when people fail to realize that they possess a problem (or, perhaps, do not believe that they can overcome it). As a result of such attitudes, people at the precontemplation stage do not seek to change their ways. In short, they are "not ready". Part of the lore of Alcoholics Anonymous, for example, states that before a process of recovery begins, alcoholics must "hit bottom" in order to realize they need to take action. Until these people recognize that a severe crisis exists (typically revealed through drastic reversals in their lives), the limbo of precontemplation is likely to exist.

Therapy at this stage (and at all phases of recovery) needs to deal with clients with reference to where they are emotionally, what they believe, and their level of motivation. If clients do not believe that they have a problem, for example, urging them to take aggressive action to combat it will fall upon deaf ears. Therapists, however, might encourage clients to keep track of the difficulties in their lives and keep an open mind about their possible causes. A heavy drinker, for example, might be asked to keep a record of how much money is spent on liquor, to notice if the problems in their lives are related to alcohol, and so forth. Those who do so might eventually begin to perceive that drinking might be an underlying cause of their difficulties. A willingness to sincerely participate in therapy often begins at that point.

In the contemplation stage, people begin to wonder if they might have a problem. Instead of seeing no connection between drinking and the troubles faced, for example, these people might begin to recognize that a relationship

120 Strategies of mitigation

exists between drinking and the unhappy situations they endure. Therapists at this stage should not rush or push people. Suggesting that help is available and providing evidence that others in a similar situation have found success, however, can help build optimum, confidence, and a willingness to participate in a program of recovery.

The preparation stage begins when people are ready to act. These people become interested in taking positive and concrete steps and doing so in the immediate, foreseeable future. Such action might begin as small and relatively unorganized steps towards their goal. During preparation, those providing psychological counseling, therapy, or advice can provide encouragement, point to possible strategies, facilitate treatment, work to eliminate barriers, and so forth. The goal is to emphasize that help is available and facilitate the client's emerging goal of recovery and actions that facilitate it.

The action stage involves people taking specific and overt steps to modify their lives and deal with their problems. During this phase, counseling, role-modeling, providing advice, and so forth can help clients to maintain their focus, develop the skills needed for success, while embracing appropriate attitudes and choices.

After effectively taking action for an extended period of time (six months is often used as a yardstick), people are said to have reached the maintenance stage. During this period, the goal involves helping people to maintain the tools needed to successfully deal with their problems as they learn to use these techniques in a more independent manner. During the action stage, for example, those being treated for alcoholism might be asked to live structured lives that are dictated by their program of therapy. Once in the maintenance stage, these requirements are systematically relaxed and the individuals become increasingly responsible for their continued sobriety. During this transition, therapists emphasize strategies of healthy living. Support groups, such as Alcoholics Anonymous, are typically recommended. The goal is for individuals to experience a smooth transition from structured treatment to a more independent lifestyle.

The termination stage occurs when people no longer have the propensity to engage in the behavior that previously caused problems. If this level is reached, all treatment and strategies for combating the malady can be eliminated. This, ultimately, is the goal: helping people get on with their lives. A rule of thumb when dealing with some people (such as alcoholics), however, is to emphasize that permanent vigilance might be needed because the threat of relapse will always exist. As a result, those who participate in AA are encouraged to remain involved with the program in order keep their vulnerability to alcohol in check.

The observation that constant caution is a good idea points to the fact that relapse is a possibility and it often occurs. Relapse involves a return to the unhealthy behaviors that were previously under control. A pattern of chronic relapse often occurs among people dealing with psychological problems and dysfunctions. Relapse is not a stage, however, it is an interruption or setback in the process of recovery.

This method and its phases are presented in Table 9–3.

Client-centered therapy **121**

TABLE 9–3 Phases in the Stages of Change Model

Issue	Description	Analysis
Precontemplation	The individual does not believe that a problem exists and/or that treatment will be beneficial.	Therapists might encourage the client to keep track of the troubles in life and what counterproductive actions accompany them.
Contemplation	The individual, although not convinced a problem exists, develops a more open mind and a willingness to objectively view their lives.	If the client becomes more objective, a readiness to consider a wider array of explanations for hurtful situations might develop. This can open the door for therapy.
Preparation	The individual recognizes the problem, decides to take action. Small preliminary steps in that regard might begin.	Once the client decides to take action, the therapist often needs to help coordinate the effort and provide encouragement.
Action	The individual sincerely takes action to address the problem.	The client and the therapist form a partnership designed to foster recovery.
Maintenance	The individual successfully addresses the issue for six months or more.	After the initial period of recovery, the client is encouraged to maintain a regimen of therapy.
Termination	After full recovery, the individual ceases all treatment and lives a normal life without therapeutic intervention.	At some point, all treatment might cease. Many people, however, continue with some form of maintenance.
Relapse	At any stage in this process, a person might revert back to their old counterproductive behavior.	It is an unfortunate fact that many people who "recover" eventually return to their old ways. This real possibility should be recognized.

DISCUSSION

Treatment and recovery, therefore, can be viewed as a number of interlocking steps. The willingness to participate at a certain level is determined by the person and what the person's thinks. Therapists need to recognize this fact and act accordingly.

A word of warning. In cases of substance abuse or addiction, the therapist might be able to objectively diagnose a particular behavior as dysfunctional and do so in an impartial and accurate manner. When dealing with the social and/or economic triggers of dysfunction, however, the issue can become more complex. The costs and benefits of different ways of life, for example, cannot always be evaluated as accurately as addiction.

Although choosing a particular lifestyle might require tradeoffs, furthermore, doing so involves personal priorities that need to be considered from a culturally

122 Strategies of mitigation

relevant perspective, not with reference to universal criteria embraced by the counselor.

Nevertheless, the Stages of Change model portrays how people can systematically embrace new ideas over a period of time. It also provides suggestions regarding how therapists and counselors can most effectively deal with clients as they really exist at a specific point in their lives.

Various methods of therapy focus upon the feelings of those receiving help. Carl Rogers, for example, strongly emphasizes a client orientation. Other techniques, such as MI, are client-centered but advocate a greater degree of leadership and direction from the therapist. Both of these options are discussed from the perspective of indigenous, ethnic, and traditional people.

The legacy of Carl Rogers

The ideas central to applying the Stages of Change model within a culturally appropriate context emphasize that psychological counseling needs to focus upon the thoughts, fears, motives, beliefs, and desires of actual people. In other words, the theories and priorities of therapists should not overshadow the feelings of those who are receiving help. The approaches championed by Carl Rogers, a legendary therapist and clinician, have long been celebrated in this regard (Rogers 1951). As a result, those who work with indigenous, ethnic, and traditional people experiencing significant change will find Rogers' perspectives to be useful.

Rogers developed a client-centered style to therapy (see Rogers 1951 for a classic articulation of this method). Eventually Rogers expanded his work to transcend therapy, leading to a generalized person-centered methodology that could be used in a variety of situations (including education). In all cases, however, Rogers' thinking centers upon understanding and serving people from their own point of view, not the inclinations of those who provide services. Due to this orientation, Rogers was a leader in the development of humanistic therapy and what amounts to an existential approach. Along with Abraham Maslow, Rogers emphasized self-actualization: a very personal striving for self-fulfillment.

The concept of self-actualization has an important role in Rogers' thinking and work. He believes that people possess goals that are deep-seated and inner directed. Achieving these objectives can be envisioned as self-actualization. In many situations, unfortunately, the conditions that people face or the society in which they live might thwart their attempts to self-actualize. When this happens, people can become frustrated, alienated, and unfulfilled, leading to psychological dysfunction.

These Rogerian perspectives are clearly in sync with this book. The concept of anomie, as developed and employed in earlier chapters, for example, describes feelings and situations that undercut the ability to self-actualize. Overcoming such obstacles has been presented as a goal.

As discussed earlier, on some occasions people whose goals are thwarted develop alternative methods and choices that might lead to self-actualization. Thus, some

Client-centered therapy **123**

reactions to anomie (such as the "innovation" option discussed by Robert Merton) might have healthy, useful, and productive outcomes. On other occasions, positive growth does not occur; opportunities for self-actualization are reduced, leading to conditions that can give rise to psychological dysfunction.

Rogers taught that when people envision or struggle towards self-actualization, they tend to juxtapose two ways by which people evaluate themselves: the "real self" and the "ideal self". The real self is how people "really are" while the ideal self is what they wish we were or hope to become.

Rogers refers to the difference between the real and the ideal selves as "incongruence". He also points out that when the degree of incongruence is significant, people have a greater chance to become emotionally and psychologically disturbed or troubled. Congruence, in contrast, is a situation where the real and ideal self are relatively in sync with each other. According to Rogers, when congruence occurs, mental problems decrease.

Note how this discussion parallels the analysis of anomie that appears earlier in this book. Anomie occurs when a peoples' way of life is profoundly and rapidly changed, leading to an inability to live according to their heritage and traditions. A feeling of being unfulfilled might arise as a result. This situation is parallel to a case of significant incongruence. When the level of anomie is high, we saw that psychological dysfunction often rises. The same situation tends to occur when the level of incongruence is pronounced.

This book has provided examples of indigenous, ethnic, and traditional people who are subjected to significant change, leading to increased incongruence between their real and ideal selves. Subsistence hunters who must move to town and work in sedentary jobs, for example, might experience profound disparity between their real and the ideal selves. Thus, they would experience incongruence. Those in such circumstances are more likely to develop psychological dysfunctions.

Many other people who are forced to alter their lifestyles due to changing circumstances are likely to experience difficulties living in their traditional manner and suffer as a result. This situation can lead to incongruence/anomie, reduced self-actualization, and result in concomitant psychological dysfunction.

People who are subjected to significant change might experience at least three different types of incongruity (Walle 2004) including: (1) people identify with the old ways but cannot live according to them because of circumstances, (2) people identify with the new ways but are held back from adequate participation with them for some reason, and (3) people find themselves alienated from both the old and the new ways of life. Each of these possibilities, in its own way, can lead to significant incongruence or anomie, leading to anxiety, suffering, and dysfunction.

An overview of relevant aspects of Rogers' work is presented in Table 9–4.

Rogers' clinical tactics are very general and broad; in addition, therapeutic relationships often continue for a long time. Nevertheless, Rogers' thinking is in line with the theory of anomie that is very useful when dealing with psychological dysfunction among indigenous, ethnic, and traditional people.

124 Strategies of mitigation

TABLE 9–4 Relevant Aspects of the Rogerian Approach

Issue	Description	Analysis
Client-centered	Rogers was a clinician who emphasized client perspectives.	Eliminate or reduce the bias of ethnocentrism by considering the client's point of view.
Self-actualization	People have broad and overarching goals they hope to achieve.	The cultural background often contributes to the objectives of self-actualization.
Congruence	The individual's "Real" vs. "Ideal" selves are relatively in sync with each other.	When congruence exists there is a greater possibility that cultural goals and self-actualization can be achieved. This can reduce dysfunction.
Incongruence	The individual's "Real" vs. "Ideal" selves are relatively out of sync with each other.	When incongruence exists there is a smaller chance that cultural goals and self-actualization are achievable. This can increase dysfunction.
Anomie	Incongruence is very similar to anomie in which people become unable to live according to their culture, heritage, and traditions.	Rogers' emphasis upon self-actualization and incongruence clearly parallels the theory of anomie and the emphasis upon its potential to trigger psychological dysfunction.
Strategies	Focus on client's needs, feelings, opinions, and so forth.	A client-centered approach that focuses upon the culture of the client can be useful in combating dysfunction.

DISCUSSION

Culture helps create the goals and motives of self-actualization. Congruence or incongruence is related to the degree to which these goals can be achieved. Incongruence is often accompanied by psychological dysfunction. When congruence exists, less dysfunction tends to occur. Techniques such as Cultural Safety and Cultural Competence can help therapists envision how clients can most effectively pursue congruence and, thereby, reduce dysfunction. This chain of thought, furthermore, parallels the discussion of anomie.

Like Sigmund Freud, Rogers allowed his clients or patients to establish the agendas to be followed and set the pace at which therapy progresses. Counseling of this type can become lengthy, undirected, and lacking in focus. Today, the typical professional regimen involves providing therapy that is (1) more directed and (2) overtly deals with specific topics. A specific timeframe, furthermore, is increasingly mandated. Even though many practitioners continue to be influenced by Rogers' client-oriented approach, the current trend is for therapy to be more structured. Another popular method of therapy is MI, which is client-centered but is more focused and therapist-directed. It will be discussed next.

Motivational interviewing

As indicated above, Rogerian therapy is client-centered. As a result, it allows those receiving treatment to have great freedom when setting agendas and establishing the therapeutic relationship in a manner of their own choosing. As a result, the tactics recommended by Rogers are often labeled "non-directive".

Although MI is concerned with client feelings, it is simultaneously dedicated to achieving specific goals. As a result, therapists work with clients in a more circumscribed, defined, and systematic manner, although client needs, opinions, vulnerabilities, and desires are taken into account.

Due to this approach, MI is able to respond to the reality that therapy tends to be more efficient and effective when it is designed to address specific, pre-defined objectives. As a result, MI is typically described as "semi-directed". Providing therapy that functions in this way has become a trend that reflects both (1) the evolution of professional therapeutic and counseling methods while (2) satisfying the demands of "third parties" that provide funding. Under these conditions and the constraints that arise from them, MI and its "semi-directed" methods are increasingly popular.

MI was initially developed by William R. Miller and Steven Rollnick as a method for treating alcohol abuse (Miller 1983). As time has gone on, its application has been extended to deal with many other issues. A detailed description of the method is presented by Miller and Rollnick (1991, 2002, 2013). Compared to non-directive counseling, MI pursues somewhat more specific goals, even though it strives to be client-centered.

A basic issue of MI involves helping people deal with the ambivalence in their lives. Alcoholics, for example, might realize that they have a problem with alcohol use, but be ambivalent about the prospects of sobriety and/or be concerned about what they might lose or be forced to give up if they quit drinking. These conflicting feelings need to be worked through in order to encourage recovery.

Although not initially designed to do so, dealing with ambivalence in this sort of therapeutic manner can be adapted to help clients cope with the opportunities and options offered by changing social and economic conditions.

In order to deal with changes in the lives and the specific goals that people harbor, MI makes good use of the Stages of Change approach (that was described earlier in this chapter). Remember, however, that indigenous, ethnic, and traditional people might legitimately prefer the status quo (or their heritage) even though therapists might presuppose that change is beneficial and should be embraced. Hopefully, cultural awareness will help clarify the thinking of therapists, leading to empathy and respect for the client's point of view. In any event, dealing with feelings of ambivalence caused by some sort of change (or potential change) is typical in MI therapy.

MI, therefore, builds upon the Stages of Change model by tailoring interventions around the point of view of the client. Does the client want change or not? A semi-directed approach can deal with such variation. Specific techniques that are

126 Strategies of mitigation

recommended by MI include showing empathy and not overtly disagreeing with the client in a confrontational manner.

At least seven key aspects of MI exists (Miller et al. 1992). They are enumerated below. The brief descriptions of these techniques have been adjusted to more effectively deal with indigenous, ethnic, and traditional peoples undergoing significant change. These techniques can be useful if the client wants to maintain the status quo or not. They are listed below:

(1) The client must develop the motivation required to make positive decisions. It does not come from the therapist.
(2) Ambivalence to change or stability must be envisioned and resolved by the client.
(3) The therapist should not attempt to directly persuade the client or actively work to resolve the ambivalence they feel.
(4) The therapist should elicit information from clients in order to help them clarify issues.
(5) The therapist helps direct and focus therapy in order to help clients examine and resolve the ambivalence they face and feel.
(6) The therapist needs to recognize that the readiness for dealing with change can fluctuate.
(7) The therapeutic relationship is most effective if it functions like a partnership or a collaborative venture in which the therapist is not the dominant force.

MI, therefore, is both semi-directed and client-oriented. It helps people deal with ambivalence connected to change. Originally, this method primarily served individuals hoping to overcome bad habits and addictions. The method, however, can be expanded to help people consider, evaluate, and cope with a wider variety of changes (including social and economic change triggered by outside intervention). Thus, the technique can be applied within a broader context, including developing coping skills related to change, anomie, and alienation.

Key techniques associated with MI include showing empathy, summarizing discussions so clients can more fully envision the impacts of their choices, and avoiding actively disagreeing with or confronting the client. Exploring discrepancies (such as regarding what people want and what actually exists) is a key tactic. If people have goals that cannot be met, this discrepancy might help clients understand the implications of their choices as well as the benefits of other options.

The ultimate evaluation, however, needs to come from the client. Thus, a choice might involve embracing economic or social development vs. maintaining the status quo by sacrificing potential benefits to maintain a traditional way of life. The counselor can help clarify the issues, but the decision rests with the people.

Thus, MI can be used to help clients consider the implications of embracing change vs. maintaining traditions. An overview of MI is presented in Table 9–5.

MI is a client-centered method of therapy that focuses upon feelings of ambiguity experienced by clients. It utilizes the Stages of Change model by acknowledging

Client-centered therapy **127**

TABLE 9–5 Useful Aspects of Motivational Interviewing

Issue	Description	Analysis
Semi-directed	A semi-directed approach allows input from the client while dealing with specific issues as required.	Although client input is vital, therapy is directed around specific issues in order to be more focused and to use funding efficiently.
Client-centered	The counselor seeks a collaborative relationship, not to dominate clients.	MI seeks to give as much freedom to clients as possible to help them exercise a degree of control over the relationship.
Ambivalence	The client's ambivalence towards change is addressed. The therapist avoids making judgments about the benefits of change or stability.	Change involves tradeoffs. Helping clients to choose the appropriate options with reference to what they want is a goal of therapy. They are often initially ambivalent.
Key techniques	Summarize, avoid confrontation, explore discrepancies, and exhibit empathy.	Seek to create a situation where the client can come to conclusions in a beneficial, rational, and objective manner.

DISCUSSION

MI provides a means of focusing the client's attention around change. Originally dealing with maladies such as addiction, it can also help people confront a wide variety of changes including those triggered by economic and social transformations. In doing so, MI can strategically compare change vs. the status quo and address the ambivalence people feel in this regard.

that people experience varying feelings regarding change (versus the status quo) as well as their motivation to change. Although MI was originally designed to deal with people who were experiencing psychological dysfunctions such as substance abuse, it can be adapted to help people undergoing, evaluating, and responding to significant social and economic change. Employing MI in this manner has a potential role in helping indigenous, ethnic, and traditional people deal with many of the challenges they face and provide a means of combating anomie.

Discussion

Increasingly, methods of therapy are acknowledging the world view and opinions of clients while simultaneously downplaying the private beliefs and orientations of therapists or counselors. One example of this trend is the growing emphasis upon Cultural Safety and Cultural Competence and the recognition that those offering advice and providing help need to overcome their ethnocentrism in order to more effectively serve distinctive people and peoples.

Cultural Safety and Cultural Competence, however, are merely one part of a movement that emphasizes providing services in ways they are reflective of clients

128 Strategies of mitigation

and what they think and feel. Starting with an analysis of Cultural Safety and Cultural Competence, this chapter discussed the Stages of Change model, the work of Carl Rogers, and MI. This non-exhaustive discussion of general tools demonstrates how techniques of therapy can be adapted for indigenous, ethnic, and traditional people who experience significant social and economic change.

These tools can be useful in helping distinctive and atypical people deal with the impacts of anomie that result from rapid change. Thus, Rogers' emphasis upon incongruence as a cause of psychological dysfunction can be used in situations involving anomie caused by change and the resulting dysfunction.

These techniques are compared in Table 9–6.

TABLE 9–6 Client-centered Approaches

Issue	Description	Analysis
Cultural Safety	Devise interactions that are culturally appropriate and minimize cohesive tactics and ploys.	If clients and practitioners have similar cultures and experiences, therapy can be more effective and empowering.
Cultural Competence	Those who seek to help people need to understand them, their culture, heritage, and way of life.	Increasingly universal strategies of therapy are being replaced with culturally sensitive alternatives.
Stages of Change	As people change, they tend to pass through stages ranging from precontemplation to a termination of efforts. Relapse is a possibility.	To be most effective, therapists need to acknowledge what their clients feel and think, including if they believe they need help or not.
Carl Rogers	Carl Rogers and his work emphasize a client orientation with an eye towards the degree to which their actual lives are congruent with their "ideal selves".	Rogers was a leader in humanistic therapy that focuses upon self-actualization. This approach can be used to deal with how a cultural background can influence wants, desires, feelings of self-worth, etc.
Motivational Interviewing	Although therapy needs to be client-oriented, some direction can be helpful. Dealing with ambivalence felt by the client can be particularly useful.	Roger's client-centered approach was not focused enough to achieve the efficiency now demanded of therapists. MI and its focus upon ambivalence can balance client feelings with therapeutic goals.

DISCUSSION

When dealing with indigenous, ethnic, and traditional people, their distinctiveness should be acknowledged and addressed. Building upon Cultural Safety and Cultural Competence, a wide number of approaches can be used to accomplish this goal. Stages of Change, the work of Carl Rogers, and Motivational Interviewing were presented as representative examples of this evolving approach. These tools can be mated with concepts such as anomie in order to deal with people experiencing change on their own terms.

Chapter 10 will showcase more specialized techniques that are adapted from Gregory Bateson's homeostasis theory and a René Girardian style of analysis. Each is adapted to deal with indigenous, ethnic, and traditional peoples. These two tools, of course, are representative and not exhaustive.

Discussion questions

(1) What is Cultural Safety? What is Cultural Competence? Compare and contrast them. How can they improve the counseling and therapeutic relationship? Why might these tools be valuable when dealing with indigenous, ethnic, and traditional peoples?

(2) What is the Stages of Change model? How does it deal with people as they really are? Why should the counselor or therapist be careful when applying it to indigenous, ethnic, and traditional clients?

(3) Carl Rogers emphasized client-centered methods. Why might they be especially important with dealing with indigenous, ethnic, and traditional people? A key to Rogers' work is his focus upon self-actualization, congruence, and incongruence. How can these issues be related to the concept of anomie that is a theme of this book? Why might doing so be important?

(4) Motivational Interviewing is described as "semi-directed". What does this mean? Why is this approach distinctive from Rogers' work? Why might such differences be important? What benefits can be derived from a semi-directed approach? How might this approach be useful or problematic when dealing with indigenous, ethnic, and traditional people?

(5) Why is it important to deal with people on their own terms? What obligations does this place on the therapist or counselor? Do you think that such an approach is particularly useful when dealing with indigenous, ethnic, or traditional peoples? Why or why not?

References

Aboriginal Nurses Association of Canada, Canadian Association of Schools of Nursing (CASN), & Canadian Nurses Association (2009). *Cultural Competence and Cultural Safety in Nursing Education: A Framework for First Nations, Inuit and Métis nursing*. Retrieved from https://www.cna-aiic.ca/~/media/cna/page-content/pdf-en/first_nations_framework_e.pdf

Baker, C. (2007). "Globalization and the Cultural Safety of an Immigrant Muslim Community." *Journal of Advanced Nursing* 57 (3): 296–305.

Cross, T. L., Bazron, B. J., Dennis, K. W. & Isaacs, M. R. (1989). *Towards a Culturally Competent System of Care: A Monograph on Effective Services for Minority Children Who Are Severely Emotionally Disturbed*. (Washington, DC: Georgetown University Child Development Center, CASSP Technical Assistance Center).

Gerlach, A. J. (2012). "A Critical Reflection on the Concept of Cultural Safety." *The Canadian Journal of Occupational Therapy* 79 (3): 151–158.

Kirmayer, L. J. (2012). "Rethinking Cultural Competence." *Transcultural Psychiatry* 49 (2): 149–164.

130 Strategies of mitigation

Miller, W. R. (1983). "Motivational Interviewing with Problem Drinkers." *Behavioral Psychotherapy* 11: 147–172.

Miller, W. R. & Rollnick, S. (1991). *Motivational Interviewing: Preparing People to Change*. (New York: Guilford Press).

Miller, W. R. & Rollnick, S. (2002). *Motivational Interviewing: Preparing People to Change* (2nd ed.). (New York: Guilford Press).

Miller, W. R. & Rollnick, S. (2013). *Motivational Interviewing: Preparing People to Change* (2nd ed.). (New York: Guilford Press).

Miller, W. R., Zweben, A., DiClemente, C. C. & Rychtarik, R. G. (1992). *Motivational Enhancement Therapy Manual*. (Washington, DC: National Institute on Alcohol Abuse and Alcoholism).

National Council for Nursing in New Zealand (2005, amended 2011). *Guidelines for Cultural Safety, the Treaty of Waitangi and Maori Health in Nursing Education and Practice*. Retrieved April 5, 2019 from pro.healthmentoronline.com/assets/Uploads/refract/pdf/Nursing_Council_cultural-safety11.pdf.

Office of Minority Health (2002). *Teaching Cultural Competence in Health Care: A Review of Current Concepts, Policies and Practices*. (Washington, DC: U. S. Department of Health and Human Services).

Prochaska, J. O. & Velicer, W. F. (1997, September–October). "The Transtheoretical Model of Health Behavior Change." *American Journal of Health Promotion* 12 (1): 38–48.

Prochaska, J. O., Velicer, W. F., Rossi, J. S., Goldstein, M. G. & Marcus, B. H. (1994, January). "Stages of Change and Decisional Balance for 12 Problem Behaviors." *Health Psychology* 13 (1): 39–46.

Rogers, C. (1951). *Client-Centered Therapy: Its Current Practice, Implications and Theory*. (London: Constable).

Thackrah, R. D. & Thompson, S. C. (2013, July 8). "Refining the Concept of Cultural Competence: Building on Decades of Progress." *The Medical Journal of Australia* 199 (1): 35–38.

Walle, Alf H. (2004). "Native People and the DSM IV-TR: Expanding Diagnostic Criteria to Reflect Minority Trauma." *Journal of Ethnicity in Substance Abuse* 3 (3): 49–65.

Wepa, D. (2015). *Cultural Safety in Aotearoa New Zealand*. (Cambridge, UK: Cambridge University Press).

Relevant terms

Action The phase of the Stages of Change model that exists when the individual is actively resolving the problems faced.

Alcoholics Anonymous A well-respected self-help group that has had a significant influence upon a wide variety of self-help groups.

Ambivalence In MI, the degree of doubt, fear, sense of possible loss, and so forth that accompanies therapy.

Client-centered therapy The client is greatly involved in planning therapy as opposed to the practitioner taking a dominant and leadership role. Carl Rogers was a major advocate.

Congruence According to Carl Rogers, situations where the real self closely parallels the ideal self.

Contemplation The phase of the Stages of Change model that exists when the individual begins to suspect that a problem exists and becomes more open-minded in that regard.

Cultural Competence Those providing help have a relevant understanding of the culture and traditions of those they seek to serve.

Client-centered therapy 131

Cultural Safety An initiative originating in New Zealand that seeks to make health care more culturally sensitive and responsive to the cultural needs of peoples.

Discrepancies In MI, a situation where people's goals are not gained by their actions.

Ideal self According to the Carl Rogers model, who people imagine they are or hope to become.

Incongruence According to the Rogers model, a big difference between the real and the ideal self.

Maintenance The phase of the Stages of Change model that exists when the individual has not exhibited the problem for an extended period of time (typically six months).

Motivational Interviewing (MI) A semi-directed method of therapy that seeks to have clients deal with the ambivalence in their lives.

Non-confrontational A key technique of MI.

Precontemplation The phase of the Stages of Change model that exists when the individual does not recognize a problem exists.

Preparation The phase of the Stages of Change model that exists when people become interested in changing their life and might take small steps in that direction.

Real self In Carl Rogers' model, people as they really are.

Relapse According to the Stages of Change model, individuals may return to their problematic behavior. This is not a stage of growth but an interruption in dealing with the problem.

Rogers, Carl A major clinical therapist who emphasized client-centered therapy.

Self-actualization A condition emphasized by Carl Rogers and Abraham Maslow that focuses upon people achieving their most personal and treasured goals.

Self-help program A program or organization in which laymen attempt to help each other.

Semi-directed Strategies of intervention in which the needs of the client are recognized and respected although the therapist exerts some control over the therapeutic relationship.

Stages of Change model A model of therapy that states that people go through various phases as they become ready to attempt recovery.

Termination The phase of the Stages of Change model that exists when the individual stops active treatment after the issue being addressed appears to be resolved.

Transtheoretical Model Another name for the Stages of Growth model.

10

REPRESENTATIVE TACTICS

Learning objectives

Chapter 9 was largely theoretical and abstract. Actual therapy, however, is specific and hands on. As a result, adapting relevant methods that can serve the needs of specific people is a key to success. Examples include reworking Gregory Bateson's theories of cybernetics and René Girard's work with role-modeling and its implications. These, of course, are but two representative examples of how existing methods can be adapted to deal with anomie and its potential impacts upon mental health. Others exist.

Discussions in this chapter include:

(1) Envisioning therapy as a tailored technique.
(2) Using Bateson's homeostasis theory to deal with a reshuffling of power and authority and the stress that can result from it.
(3) Employing a Girardian analysis to address the impact of changing and/or competing role models.
(4) Connecting these techniques with concepts such as anomie, culture loss, and alienation.
(5) Using these examples to indicate how to better serve indigenous, ethnic, and traditional peoples.

Introduction

Building upon Cultural Safety and Cultural Competence, Chapter 9 dealt with a number of general therapeutic methods including the Stages of Change model, the client-oriented therapy of Carl Rogers, and MI. Such tools can help therapists transcend ethnocentrism and an unawareness of client perspectives. These tools

Representative tactics **133**

can also facilitate clients setting their own agendas, goals, and priorities in ways that can relieve alienation, anomie, and dysfunction.

In Chapter 10, the discussion becomes more precise and practitioner-oriented. Specifically, the works of Gregory Bateson and René Girard are showcased as particular examples that demonstrate how specialized techniques can be reworked with the needs of distinctive populations in mind. These examples, of course, are representative and not exhaustive. Many other tools can (and should) be transformed in order to more effectively deal with indigenous, ethnic, and traditional people who are subjected to change, stress, and anomie.

Homeostasis theory

Gregory Bateson (1904–1980) was a prominent ethnographer who participated in the "golden age" of anthropological fieldwork before becoming involved with mental health issues. In the 1930s, Bateson conducted extensive studies among indigenous people in New Guinea and Bali, collaborating with his wife, legendary ethnographer Margaret Mead. During World War II, Bateson contributed to covert OSS activities in Burma and Thailand and was also involved in The United States Office of Strategic Services (OSS) sponsored missions in China, India, and Ceylon.

After his wartime activities, Bateson became involved with cybernetics: the discipline that studies how systems are regulated and the role that communication plays in that process. The celebrated "father" of cybernetics is Norbert Weiner (1894–1964), who wrote the seminal text on the subject: *Cybernetics, or Control and Communication in the Animal and the Machine* (1948). Building upon such pioneering work, Bateson combined cybernetics with his background in anthropology. In *Steps to an Ecology of Mind* (1972), Bateson systematically adapted cybernetic theory in a manner that is relevant to anthropology, the social sciences, and humanistic activities.

A key component in cybernetics is the "feedback loop" in which behavior within a system adjusts itself in order to maintain stability. The classic example of a feedback loop, of course, is the thermostat in a heater. The goal of the device is to maintain a stable temperature. When the heat gets too high, the thermostat sends a signal to turn the heater off. As a result, the space begins to cool. After the temperature lowers to a certain level, the thermostat sends another signal that turns the heater back on. As a result of gathering information and responding to it, the heater maintains the temperature at a relatively constant level. This process of self-regulation is known as homeostasis. In addition to serving machines, the feedback mechanisms of homeostasis can also maintain and regulate the relationships between people. Social groups often adapt and respond in accordance with such cybernetic routines in the overt or covert quest to stabilize social systems and the lives of people impacted by them.

As Bateson's career matured, he became increasingly interested in combining cybernetics with theories of mental health and psychological therapy. The concept of homeostasis became a key component of Bateson's research as he adapted it to portray how people deal with the pain, disruption, and restructuring caused by stress and change.

134 Strategies of mitigation

Bateson's work regarding what he calls "family homeostasis" models how a family stabilizes itself when coping with the disruption caused by the alcoholism or drug addiction of one of its members. Bateson notes that although these tactics might have benefits, negative long-term ramifications (or at least stresses) might simultaneously occur.

Bateson's conception of family homeostasis can be easily presented.

(1) When people fall into a pattern of addiction, they often lose the ability to act in a responsible and predictable manner.
(2) As a result of their dysfunction, addicts typically become ineffectual and unable to make fruitful decisions and/or assume their usual leadership roles within the family.
(3) Due to this incapacity, power and decision-making clout within the family is shifted away from addicts to others who are more responsible. Doing so maintains a degree of stability or homeostasis within the family. Thus, in order to compensate for problems brought on by addiction, spouses and children take over functions and responsibilities that were previously the realm of the now-incompetent addict.
(4) Even though the family is changed, from a homeostatic point of view stabilization takes place because it continues to exist and function. In this fashion, the family is maintained and its structures and functions are preserved (although transformed in some ways).

So far, so good: the structure of the family is preserved, although altered. New problems, however, can arise if the alcoholic or addict recovers, because:

(5) After recovery, previously incapacitated addicts typically seek to reclaim their legitimate positions of authority within the family that had been lost or seized by others when the addicts were dysfunctional. Reclaiming these roles and rights, however, is often complicated and difficult because the family power structure and decision-making protocols have typically been transformed, stripping the addict of authority and clout.
(6) After this power shift takes hold, family members who gained power and freedom during the addicts' dysfunctional phase often hesitate to surrender these gains, leading to tensions, confusion, and hard feelings.

Spouses who became comfortable making decisions unilaterally, for example, often regret the potential loss of authority. Children who relish the greater freedom they gained when the addict was inattentive and non-assertive might begrudge the reestablishment of normal parental controls, causing disruptive disagreements to arise. As a result,

(7) Strife within the family might grow, possibly to the point of giving the addict inadvertent and/or covert encouragement to relapse. These tendencies can be a barrier to long-term recovery.

Bateson et al. (1956) developed the concept of the *double bind*. Although they did so while researching schizophrenia, Bateson emphasized that such communication issues are commonplace. In layman's terms, a double bind occurs when people are put into a situation where they are "damned if they do and damned if they don't".

Consider the family homeostasis example provided above. On the one hand, family members want their addicted loved one to recover and become accountable and dependable. Therefore, addicts are urged to cease their addictive behavior, and start being more responsible. On the other hand, addicts who work hard at recovery will seek to reassert their legitimate role within the family. Doing so, however, will potentially impinge upon the de facto power structure that emerged to compensate for the addicts' former erratic behavior. Being asked to surrender this authority might be resented and opposed.

Due to the full range of ramifications associated with recovery, sober and responsible behavior often conflicts with the transformed family structure and the actual decision-making protocols that have come to exist. Thus, the reshuffling of power caused by the addicts' renaissance can be stressful and cause problems. Although family members overtly applaud the addicts' recovery, they are apt to be covertly resentful and lament the losses they must bear as recovery takes hold. This situation can create a classic example of the double bind.

An overview of Bateson's thinking is portrayed in Table 10–1.

TABLE 10–1 Bateson's Family Homeostasis Theory

Issue	Description	Analysis
Cybernetics	Cybernetics studies systems as well as the communication and protocols of control within systems.	Although cybernetics can explain how machines function, it can also model how social systems and people operate.
Homeostasis	A key aspect of cybernetics explores how systems regulate and sustain themselves.	Social systems need to maintain themselves function effectively. Homeostatic mechanisms can help facilitate doing so.
Double bind	A "damned if you do, damned if you don't" situation where people will fail or disappoint no matter what they do.	If placed in a situation where whatever choice they make unsatisfactory, a "no win" situation arises.
Family homeostasis	Families suffering from addiction can demonstrate how homeostasis and the double bind can be unhealthy.	Families under stress adapt to maintain themselves. Reversing these adaptations can lead to stress and resistance.

DISCUSSION

Bateson's theory of family homeostasis is a classic example of using cybernetics to model and deal with psychological problems and concomitant dysfunction within social systems, such as families. Originally developed to deal with addiction, its application can be expanded.

136 Strategies of mitigation

Although Bateson's family homeostasis theory focuses upon addiction, dysfunction, and family adjustment, its basic elements can be adapted to explore how other conditions might undermine a person's effectiveness, resulting in power struggles. Such an adaptation can be used when dealing with the stress that accompanies economic development and/or the social and psychological dysfunction it potentially causes.

Adapting the homeostasis model

Although Bateson's family homeostasis model was developed to deal with addiction (a specific application), it can be adapted and expanded to serve in a broader context. Such an adaptation might take the following form:

(1) When specific people gain and/or lose power, transformations of the social systems are likely to occur. In addition to mental and psychological issues, social and economic shifts can be involved.
(2) When some people lose power due to social and economic changes, others tend to gain power, resources, and authority.
(3) Those who lose power, the respect of others, and so forth, often seek to regain it. This process can be seen as an example of homeostasis in which attempts are made to return to a former state of stability that existed in the past.
(4) Those who usurp power, resources, and respect during a period of change typically want to preserve their gains and will resist a return to the former status quo. Doing so is a homeostatic response that seeks to maintain the advantages made.

Thus, two distinct homeostatic responses exist and they directly conflict with one another. People who lose power want to regain it. Those who have gained power want to keep it. Each stakeholder seeks to maintain some sort of equilibrium in a homeostatic fashion. This situation can:

(5) Result in double binds affecting either and/or both groups.

Traditionalists believe their heritage is important and they lament power shifts and evolving trends in social and economic life that undercut this legacy. On the other hand, those favoring change often conclude that the past is holding people back. Such conflicts can easily lead to tension. Thus, some local people might advocate the preservation of tradition while others encourage change. These conflicting messages can take an emotional toll. In addition, power struggles between the traditionalists and progressives potentially lead to hurtful conflict.

Progressives, who hope to transform society, can also find themselves in a double bind if they believe that they have much to contribute, but fear that a renaissance of tradition is poised to undercut their progress. In both cases, rival systems of homeostasis can act in conflict with each other.

Thus, homeostatic struggles can result from power swings, not merely from dysfunctions such as addiction. These shifts, furthermore, might trigger dysfunction among those who were not dysfunctional until exposed to the stress and pain of change. When conditions evolve, winners and losers emerge. Winners have gained something and, typically, they want to keep it. Traditionalists, in contrast, often seek to replicate or preserve the social and economic relationships they value. Care must be exercised if self-determinism is to occur in an orderly and non-disruptive manner. This can be a difficult goal.

Thus, Bateson's homeostatic model can be expanded and generalized to deal with the disruption caused by any changes that lead to power reallocations (and the tensions and dysfunctions resulting from it).

The more generalized homeostasis model is abstracted in Table 10–2.

Bateson is a major anthropologist who emerged as an important force in the study of psychological dysfunction. His work demonstrates how shifts in power can cause tensions and dysfunctions to increase.

Having dealt with Bateson and his theories of cybernetics and homeostasis, the discussion will continue with an analysis of the work of René Girard, another anthropologically-inspired theorist who is most identified with literary-based cultural analysis.

TABLE 10–2 General Homeostasis Theory

Issue	Description	Analysis
Power shifts	Changing situations can result in power shifts involving various people and groups.	Culture and economic change creates winners and losers. Power shifts are the inevitable result.
Tension results	If shifts in power take place, tensions can develop.	When some gain and others lose, strains can emerge that need to be resolved.
Relationship stress	As tensions take hold, the stress felt by people can grow.	Unmitigated tension can lead to stress in people and their relationships.
Dysfunction	Social and psychological dysfunction can arise from tension and stress.	Tension and stress can be a catalyst leading to dysfunction in individuals and society.
Resolution	Reducing or mitigating tension and stress can lessen dysfunction.	Because stress and tension can cause dysfunction, mitigating it can reduce social and psychological problems.

DISCUSSION

By generalizing Bateson's family homeostasis theory, it can deal with a wide variety of situations (1) where people lose power and authority and (2) social tensions and psychological dysfunctions result from these changes. As a result, an expanded homeostasis model can deal with the impacts of economic change.

138 Strategies of mitigation

Girardian analysis

Gregory Bateson, as discussed previously, was an anthropologist who studied how social structures (and the relationships created by them) respond to changing family conditions. In adapting such ideas to deal with economic development and psychological dysfunction, his model was generalized to deal with a wider range of rivalries and power shifts that might coincide with social and economic development.

In addition to social structural models (such as Bateson's), alternative paradigms, such as "mental structuralism", examine innate psychological universals and their influences (see Chapter 5 of my *Rethinking Business Anthropology: Cultural Strategies in Marketing and Management* (Walle 2013) for a discussion of mental structuralism). Sigmund Freud, a well-known mental structuralist, developed intuitive theories regarding the origins of culture and the principles underlying social life. Freud went on to make a variety of speculations regarding the origins of human culture, and he intuitively viewed social relationships from that vantage point. René Girard, a literary critic turned anthropologically oriented social and psychological theorist, follows a similar path.

Girard's style of reasoning gives rise to an array of intriguing concepts that, like Freud's anthropological work, lacks a robust methodological foundation. In other words, his theories are not backed up by the usual standards of evidence. This is true even though Girard asserts his work is empirical and grounded upon credible evidence. In this regard, Girard observes, "Our theory should be approached, then, as one approaches any scientific hypothesis" (1977, 316).

In spite of this insistence, Girard's methodology fails to adhere to the usual standards of rigorous and robust investigation. (For an analysis of qualitative methods, see my *Qualitative Research in Business: A Practical Overview* (Walle 2015).) Such observations are not made to condemn Girard's work, but merely to point to what it is and what it is not.

Girard can also be criticized with reference to the techniques of modern cross-cultural anthropology. A key challenge to the credibility of much cross-cultural and comparative analysis is "Galton's Problem" that observes that parallels and similarities among cultures might merely result from diffusion, not some innate influence or tendency, such as human universals or archetypes (see Narroll 1965). These observations are not made merely to critique Girard, but to better showcase the point of view of the present monograph which focuses upon specific cultural influences, not inherent or universal phenomena, such as "human nature".

Girard's analysis of *Don Quixote* in his first book, *Deceit, Desire, and the Novel* (1961–1976), provides an excellent example of the general model and method that he develops. Girard notes that Quixote spends his life imitating Amadís de Gaula in the hopes of duplicating him and his heroics. The story of de Guala was popular in the early 16th century and was a well-known component of Spanish popular culture. Castilian author Garci Rodriguez de Montalvo gathered and edited the stories that were circulating about this legendary hero and contributed his own additions to them. (The earliest surviving printing is dated 1508.) These tales were circulated widely during the early 16th century. Miguel de Cervantes wrote Don Quixote, using the heroic de Guala as the foil for his comic hero: a would-be knight who views de Guala as a role model to be imitated and emulated.

Girard labels the process of one person influencing the desires or inclinations of another as "mediation". Thus, Amadís emerges as a mediator or role model to be copied. In Cerventes' novel, Quixote experiences many troubles and misadventures that derive from this envy and his habit of copying de Gaula. Girard calls such negative copying mimesis. He refers to mediation between those who are in some sort of close contact or conflict as "internal mediation". When this is the case, tensions, rivalries, and struggles potentially develop. Expanding his vision beyond literary criticism, Girard sees such a process as commonplace and occurring cross-culturally in a variety of contexts.

In *Violence and the Sacred* (1972), Girard expanded his thinking to incorporate anthropology, folklore, mythology, as well as ancient Greek tragedies. Girard used this monograph to extend and broaden his theories of mimesis. Written while a faculty member at the State University of New York at Buffalo, and a colleague of culturally oriented critic Leslie Fiedler and noted folklorist Bruce Jackson, overt borrowing from such thinkers is not obvious. Nonetheless, subtle parallels exist (such as a humanistic and cross-cultural emphasis upon massive and overarching cultural forces).

Exploring an array of primitive societies in a manner that is similar to Freud's cultural conjectures, Girard points to mechanisms that help stabilize society. Specifically, Girard argues that the social order in primitive societies is often linked to efforts to control rivalry and conflict through a process of scapegoating which is regulated by religion.

Ironically, while Girard was at Buffalo, Raoul Narroll (another colleague at his university in the anthropology department) was developing world-class methods regarding how to conduct state of the art cross-cultural anthropological research. Girard was made aware of these options, but he did not incorporate them into his work (Walle personal communication 2015a).

Relevant aspects of Girard's theories can be presented as:

(1) Copying others is a common human activity. Some of this borrowing is merely ad hoc imitation that often has useful and beneficial results. Education and training, for example, frequently involve the student imitating the teacher or mentor.

(2) Other types of copying, however, can exert negative influences. Girard refers to harmful examples of copying as mimesis to distinguish the undesirable or hurtful implications of copying and/or counterproductively duplicating the desires or habits that others display. Girard emphasizes that, as a result of copying these role models, people become similar and adopt parallel desires. As an example, Girard points to the ancient Greek story of Oedipus who, as you might recall, fell in love with his mother (duplicating the desires of his father) and

140 Strategies of mitigation

paid a terrible price as a result. Girard saw a pattern of hurtful mimetic desires being chronicled in great literature. He later made an investigation of folklore and mythology in an attempt to extend his perspectives. This research further refined Girard's theory of mimetic conflict in which emerging sameness, created by copying, leads to tension and dysfunctional responses.

(3) Girard continues by suggesting that the resulting frustration and rivalry that stems from the tensions created by mimesis (hurtful copying) can lead to strife in the community. This conflict needs to be reduced. By lessening these tensions, social and economic life can function more smoothly and effectively.

(4) Girard went on to assert that a degree of harmony is often reestablished by what he refers to as "scapegoating", in which the entire community rallies together to oppress, punish, or kill some (perhaps innocent) individuals in ways that reduce tensions and, thereby, stabilize and/or bring peace to the community. According to Girard, the mechanism of the scapegoat has been used to reduce tensions since ancient times. Its process involves blaming problems and tensions upon some individual or group and focusing the community's anger and vengeance against it. When this occurs, other causes of strife can be overlooked as the community collectively blames the scapegoat. Due to the resulting unity, a degree of harmony can be restored to a community that otherwise would suffer from chaotic tensions.

Girard further expands his theories in ways that (among other characteristics) present a specific interpretation of Christianity, but these components of his work (although rich and insightful) are not relevant within the present context. The perspective here, furthermore, deals with responses as social in nature (and not necessarily fueled by inherent or innate aspects of humanity as Girard suggests and emphasizes).

So adapted and adjusted, Girard's model is abstracted in Table 10–3.

Although not originally designed to do so, Girard's basic approach, like Bateson's, can be adjusted to deal with the broader ramifications of social and economic change.

A community undergoing a significant transformation (or a candidate for it) must deal with the pros and cons of the status quo vs. the costs and benefits of proceeding in a new direction. Thus, situations involving change and stability can create rival role models with diverse backgrounds. When larger groups, such as communities, are in contact, this imitation might be part of a larger process of cultural diffusion that can include (1) economic methods, (2) the products consumed, (3) the current level of knowledge, tastes, world views, and so forth. If what Girard depicts as mere ad hoc imitation takes place, minimal negative ramifications might result.

Other role-modeling and/or cultural diffusion, in contrast, might possess hurtful potentials at least for some segment of the population. When this is true, the community might divide into rival camps (as we saw with Bateson's work). They can often be categorized as "traditionalists" and "progressives" or some similar dichotomy.

TABLE 10-3 A Basic Girardian Model

Issue	Description	Analysis
Imitation	People tend to copy each other. Some imitation is positive.	A basic and recurring reaction or activity of people is to copy role models.
Mimesis	Some copying exerts negative influences and/or can build tensions. Hurtful and disruptive potentials can result.	Copying can (1) make people similar (2) in ways that make their desires parallel. If so, rivalry and conflict can result.
Strife	Rivalry and competition (products of mimesis) can lead to strife and tension when people have similar motives.	Similarities can lead to internal mediation that generates jealousy, potentially leading to violence and anger.
Scapegoating	By eliminating an individual or group that is viewed as the source of conflict and tension, strife can be reduced leading to greater harmony within the community.	Societies and communities need harmony in order to function effectively. Collectively dealing with a universally hated scapegoat can help to achieve this goal.

DISCUSSION

Girard seeks to deal with innate human response, or even instinctual phenomena (as Freud had done in his social and anthropological theorizing). Although Girard's mental structuralism is rejected here, a modified Girardian model can be reworked to reflect social structural responses. His work is discussed from this perspective.

If this division is deep and antagonistic, each faction might envision its own variety of scapegoat. Traditionalists tend to assume that the problems with life and society stem from changes that are taking place within the economy and community. These people can easily view the forces of change and its advocates as scapegoats that need to be removed, shunned, or rejected.

The progressive forces, in contrast, usually feel that those who cling to the old ways are archaic, reactionary, and holding the community back. In their mind, supporters of the heritage and its traditions emerge as scapegoats who are viewed as creating misery who must be removed or controlled.

This situation of rivals poised in opposition to each other might continue in a dialectal fashion (in line with the thinking of G. W. F. Hegel and Karl Marx). According to dialectical reasoning, tradition can be depicted as the *thesis* with progressive choices emerging as the *antithesis*. These rival and incompatible forces will struggle in conflict until some form of compromise or *synthesis* relieves the tensions. Until then, distinctive forms of scapegoating by both factions is a strong possibility. These possibilities are abstracted in Table 10–4.

As was discussed with Gregory Bateson's work, power struggles can result from and potentially cause dysfunction. Girard's contributions, in their own way, can be

142 Strategies of mitigation

TABLE 10–4 Girardian Analysis and Change

Issue	Description	Analysis
Change	Social and economic change takes place in ways that require adjustment.	Change, its costs, and benefits can influence role models.
Memetic response	Counterproductive copying can either embrace tradition or change.	Hurtful emulation of both tradition and change can prompt mimetic responses.
Traditional scapegoat	Those embracing change are likely to depict traditionalists as scapegoats to be cast out.	Those embracing tradition are depicted as passé, reactionary, out of touch, and, thereby, emerge as scapegoats.
Progressive scapegoat	The traditionalists, in contrast, are likely to portray the agents of change as scapegoats.	Costs and disruptions accompanying change are emphasized in ways that make progressive people scapegoats.
Dysfunction	Due to scapegoating and its implications, dysfunction at personal and societal levels can occur.	People who have been turned into scapegoats can face pressures that are alienating and lead to dysfunction.
Reconciliation	If the tensions between factions weakens, rival scapegoating can be reduced and dysfunction can be more effectively controlled.	The dialectical process of thesis, antithesis, and synthesis can facilitate a resolution of differences and/or a reconciliation that reduces dysfunction.

DISCUSSION

Social and economic change can trigger significant dysfunction, stemming, in part, from the blame and antagonism that traditionalists and progressives feel towards each other. This can lead to psychological pain and possible dysfunction. Counterproductive scapegoating can result. A revision of Girard's theory of mimesis, coupled with dialectical analysis, can be used to model this process.

interpreted in a similar manner. Mimesis can lead to a variety of people exhibiting parallel needs and wants. This can result in a power struggle for control. Mimesis and infighting that result can be viewed as an artifact that involves the tensions involved with borrowing from others vs. maintaining traditions. As a result of emulating outsiders, people can lose track of who they are if, for example, they uncritically begin to embrace the lifestyles of dominating outsiders. The resulting alienation can be another source of dysfunction.

Thus, both Bateson's and Girard's work can provide clues regarding social change, economic development, and dysfunction. This can be especially true when cultural, social, and economic diffusion leads to mimetic borrowing that potentially triggers dysfunction among indigenous, ethnic, and traditional people who are subjected to profound intrusive influences.

Girard's theories of mimesis and scapegoating can be adapted to deal with situations in which indigenous, ethnic, and traditional people face significant changes. In order to do so, Girard's mental structural approach has been transformed to deal with social structural situations, not merely human universals.

Emil Zola (Brown 1995) was a great French writer with profound insights. He was also a strong advocate of phrenology, a debunked psychological paradigm. In his preface of La Fortune des Rougon, (Zola 1871), for example, Zola observes that he intends to study "the slow succession of accidents pertaining to the nerves or the blood [psychological transformation through time], which befall a race . . . [and] determine in each individual . . . feelings, desires and passions . . . all the natural and instinctive manifestations". Even though Zola did so with reference to discredited and misinformed psychological paradigms, the portrayals of his characters hold up and have withstood the test of time. Thus, Zola's writing rings true even though it is based on faulty reasoning and pseudoscience.

This ironic observation can be applied to Girard as well. Girard based his theories upon a foundation that possesses weak empirical support and is of questionable accuracy. Nonetheless, many of Girard's interpretations are useful as ad hoc observations regarding how people actually behave. Girard, for example, emphasized that people learn from others and copy what these people do and feel. Some imitation is good while other examples (dubbed mimesis by Girard) are hurtful and counterproductive. These tendencies are often showcased when indigenous, ethnic, and traditional people are subjected to profound change. Under these circumstances, internal tensions within the community often arise, encouraging rival camps (that champion tradition and change respectively) to sacrifice distinctive scapegoats in ways that reflect their points of view. If the differences between these rival camps are resolved, reconciliation and harmony can potentially result. The process of dialectics is one way of envisioning this process.

Discussion

A key concept of this book is anomie. It emphasizes that if people are subjected to profound and unregulated change, they can suffer from alienation and be cut off from their way of life and its traditions. This situation can emerge as a breeding ground for dysfunction. Throughout this book, methods of mitigating anomie have been discussed.

Continuing such a line of reasoning, this chapter discusses how existing models can be transformed to deal with social change and its impacts upon indigenous, ethnic, and traditional peoples. Gregory Bateson was a respected anthropologist who combined the social sciences with information theory (or cybernetics). Bateson found this combination could be of value when dealing with psychological dysfunction and evolving family structures. Although Bateson's model was designed to deal with the effects of substance abuse upon relatively small social units, his ideas can be adapted to deal with change, stress, and dysfunction caused by broader social and/or economic interventions as well as transformations caused by them.

144 Strategies of mitigation

An expansion of Bateson's homeostasis model can be used to deal with the process of anomie and how it impacts people. Due to social, technological, and economic changes, power shifts can occur which influence authority, respect, and recognition within the community. These trends can advance the cause of progressive people who embrace the new ways. On many occasions, however, the forces of tradition and the heritage of the community experience a resurgence of authority and respect. When this happens, the progressives who have gained power will hesitate to relinquish it. The resulting strains within the community can lead to tension and dysfunction. In all of these processes, homeostasis works towards restoring and preserving the social unit even while changing it.

While Bateson was a respected anthropologist who examined social structures and relationships, René Girard used literary analysis to analyze innate and universal aspects of humanity. Like Claude Lévi-Strauss, Girard can be described as a "mental structuralist" because his work explores human nature, not distinctive cultures or peoples. By reworking Girard's theories to emphasize cultures and their structures, his work was adapted to deal with indigenous, ethnic, and traditional people experiencing change.

Girard emphasizes the importance of copying. When cultures and economic systems collide, social disruption or anomie often occurs. Under such conditions, some people continue to replicate the old ways of tradition. This process may become mimetic (or hurtful copying) if clinging to the past puts people at a social, economic, or emotional disadvantage.

Others may embrace the new innovations or options that are offered. These options can emerge as mimesis if, by doing so, people reject their heritage by emulating new options in a hurtful manner and/or if they are not able to adequately participate in the way of life they seek to embrace (the basic compliant of Frantz Fanon in *Black Skins, White Masks*).

To deal with people in appropriate and effective ways, they need to be understood on their own terms. In this monograph, several references have been made to the fact that if advisors to indigenous, ethnic, and traditional people are blinded by their own visions, effectively serving these people becomes difficult, if not impossible. This chapter provides examples of how the needs and wants of distinctive peoples can be more effectively taken into account.

Cultural Safety and Cultural Competence emphasize that understanding the client's heritage and way of life is vital. Advisors who lack this foundation are apt to make profound errors and misjudgments. By being culturally aware and by understanding what people feel and want, the emotional and intellectual background needed to provide effective service can be established. In Chapter 9, these observations led to a discussion of the "client-centered" approach initially associated with figures such as Carl Rogers and eventually reworked in more focused forms of therapy, such as MI.

The goals of Cultural Safety, Cultural Competence, and client-centered approaches fit well with the methods of Bateson and Girard. Gregory Bateson's homeostasis model examined changing power relationships and how they can

Representative tactics **145**

impact the dealings between people in hurtful ways. The work of René Girard, in a somewhat similar fashion, deals with the disruptive force of rivalry and how hurtful scapegoating can arise. Both of these models can be tailored to deal with indigenous, ethnic, and traditional people.

These two approaches, of course, are representative and non-exhaustive. Nevertheless, they show how economic and social change can trigger dysfunction.

The range of approaches discussed is presented in Table 10–5.

It is hoped that the reader will recognize that these adaptations are illustrative and not exhaustive. Many other theories can be reworked to serve indigenous, ethnic, and traditional people that are experiencing change and the trauma it can bring. Hopefully, the toolkit used to help indigenous, ethnic, and traditional people deal with change and its ramifications will be expanded in useful, compelling, and fruitful ways.

TABLE 10–5 Representative Approaches

Issue	Description	Analysis
Basic orientation	Adopting views that reflect the culture and heritage of clients.	Distinctive people need to be treated in appropriate ways.
Anomie	Alienation and disorientation typically cause trauma among those effected by them.	Dealing with cultural change, the stress it brings, and the anomie it causes is vital when dealing with dysfunction.
Homeostasis theory	Conditions exist where some people gain power and others lose. These transitions can trigger situations that are problematic and need to be addressed.	Power struggles often take place. The resulting tensions can impact the effectiveness of therapy. Problems of this sort can arise during periods of rapid social and economic change.
Girardian analysis	Tensions spawned by rivalry can be reduced by blaming someone and unifying the community in this way.	Although the Girardian paradigm deals with human universals, it can be adapted for specific cultures and conditions.
Other alternatives	These models are representative, not exhaustive. Others can potentially be adapted to deal with the disruptions caused by change.	These two methods are the "tip of the iceberg". Although methods vary, they need to accept people as they are, downplaying therapist orientations.

DISCUSSION

Techniques such as homeostasis theory and Girardian analysis can be adapted to deal with indigenous, ethnic, and traditional people. Building upon Cultural Safety and Cultural Competence, these methods demonstrate how practitioners can respond to people in appropriate ways. When dealing with indigenous, ethnic, and traditional people, this kind of orientation can be invaluable.

146 Strategies of mitigation

Discussion questions

(1) In Chapter 9, a number of issues were discussed in order to develop client-centered therapy. How does doing so establish a foundation for Chapter 10? How can this client-centered approach be especially useful when dealing with indigenous, ethnic, and traditional peoples? How does Chapter 10 build upon the client-centered approach of Chapter 9?

(2) What is cybernetics? Why is cybernetics important when dealing with social systems? Discuss Gregory Bateson as an anthropologist who bridged the social sciences and communication theory. Why might his work be important when dealing with dysfunction?

(3) What is family homeostasis theory? How does it deal with a reshuffling of power and authority within the family? Do you believe this theory can be adapted to deal with a wide range of power relationships involving social and economic change? Do you find this approach can be useful when dealing with indigenous, ethnic, and traditional people? Why or why not?

(4) René Girard deals with a process of copying that potentially has negative implications. How can this process lead to tensions? According to Girard, what is the role of scapegoating and why is it important in dealing with tensions between people? Do you feel this theory can be adapted to deal indigenous, ethnic, and traditional people undergoing change?

(5) Are the theories of Bateson and Girard compatible with the concept of anomie discussed throughout this book? Why or why not? Do the examples of Bateson and Girard point to ways in which other theories can be adapted to deal with the issues of psychological dysfunction among indigenous, ethnic, and traditional people undergoing significant change?

References

Bateson, G., Don Jackson, D. D., Haley, J. & Weakland, J. (1956). "Toward a Theory of Schizophrenia." *Behavioral Science* 1: 251–264.

Brown, F. (1995). *Zola: A Life.* (New York City: Farrar, Straus & Giroux).

Cervantes, M. de (1548 and thereafter). *Don Quixote.* (Innumerable editions).

Girard, R. (1961–1976). *Deceit Desire and the Novel.* (Baltimore, MA: Johns Hopkins University Press; the original French version was published in 1961, the English translation in 1976).

Girard, R. (1977). *Violence and the Sacred*, translated by Patrick Gregory. (Baltimore, MA: Johns Hopkins University Press; the original French version was published in 1972).

Motalvo, G. R. de (1508). *Amadis de Guala.* Many versions published. The earlier surviving copy dates to 1508.

Naroll, R. (1965). "Galton's Problem: The Logic of Cross Cultural Research." *Social Research* 32: 428–451.

Walle, Alf H. (2013). *Rethinking Business Anthropology: Cultural Strategies in Marketing and Management.* (Yorkshire: Greenleaf Publications).

Walle, Alf H. (2015). *Qualitative Research in Business: A Practical Overview.* (Newcastle: Cambridge Scholars Publishing).

Walle, Alf H. (2015a), Personal Communication. Walle was a graduate student at the State University of Buffalo who studied both anthropology and English in the last 1960s and 1970s. He attended numerous lectures by Girard and told him about Narroll and his work.

Wiener, N. (1948). *Cybernetics, or Control and Communication in the Animal and the Machine.* (Cambridge, MA: MIT Press).

Zola, E. (1871). "Preface." In: *La Fortune des Rougon.* Original text in French available at Wikisource, translated text by the Project Gutenberg. Retrieved from https://www.gutenberg.org

Relevant terms

Antithesis   According to dialectical reasoning, the rebuttal of the thesis.

Bateson, Gregory   A social anthropologist who embraced cybernetics and developed the theory of family homeostasis.

Cybernetics   A theory of communication and control.

Deceit, Desire, and the Novel   Book by René Girard that introduces his theory of mimesis which involves hurtfully copying other people.

Dialectics   A theory of logic and evolution that pits different forces in opposition to each other in ways that lead to change and reconciliation.

Double bind   A situation in which a person is "damned if you do, damned if you don't", leaving the individual with no viable or attractive option.

Family homeostasis   A model developed by Gregory Bateson that deals with how power relationships in the family adjust in order to deal with the incapacity of one of its members.

Feedback loop   Using communication in ways that self-regulate a system.

Girard, René   Literacy critic and mental structuralist who developed theories of mimetic imitation and scapegoating.

Homeostasis   A term of cybernetics that deals with self-regulation.

Human nature   Innate aspects of humanity studied by mental structuralists.

Imitation   According to René Girard, imitation is positive copying, as opposed to mimesis, which is negative copying.

Mental structuralism   Focusing upon the inherent nature of the human mind, not the structures of society.

Mimesis   A term used by René Girard to depict hurtful imitation or copying.

Narroll, Raoul   An important cross-cultural anthropologist who dealt with methodological issues, such as taking the impact of diffusion into account.

Phrenology   A debunked theory of psychology embraced by French novelist Emil Zola.

Progressive scapegoat   A scapegoat used by traditionalists to embrace that is based on change.

Reconciliation   The process of overcoming scapegoats by both traditionalists and progressives.

Scapegoating   According to René Girard, encouraging social solidarity through the process of blaming someone/something and killing or casting it out.

Social structuralism   Focusing upon the nature of society, not innate aspects of humanity.

Synthesis   In dialectical reasoning, a reconciliation of the thesis and antithesis.

Thesis   According to dialectical reasoning, the original premise or issue under investigation.

Traditional scapegoat   The scapegoat embraced by progressives that is based on tradition.

Violence and the Sacred   A book by René Girard that expands his theory of mimesis and deals with scapegoating.

Weiner, Norbert   The father of cybernetics.

Zola, Emil   French novelist who based his characters on phrenology, a debunked theory of psychology.

EPILOGUE TO SECTION 3

Although theories, models, and paradigms provide insights, the actual methods that are used to help people need to be practitioner-oriented. Section 3 provides suggestions in that regard.

Cultural Safety and Cultural Competence emphasize that understanding those being served is an essential skill. Unfortunately, many counselors and therapists are uninformed and/or possess ethnocentric views that can undercut their ability to be effective when dealing with certain peoples. By developing the skills needed to understand and respond to people on their own terms, this limitation can be mitigated.

In addition to gaining insights regarding the client's cultural heritage, understanding the personal and idiosyncratic feelings of specific individuals is also important. Particular individuals, for example, vary in their degree of enthusiasm and/or their willingness to embrace various options. Although the abilities associated with Cultural Safety and Cultural Competence can be helpful when dealing with people, understanding the varying attitudes of specific individuals also needs to be considered.

Increasingly, however, other constraints involving time and money seek to make therapy more efficient. This trend is causing client-directed therapy to be replaced by programs of treatment that are more semi-structured, providing practitioners with a greater a role in directing the therapeutic relationship and the topics addressed. MI is an example of doing so.

With these perspectives in mind, two representative approaches were discussed: Gregory Bateson's homeostasis model and René Girard's work with mimesis (or hurtful imitation). By adapting these methods to deal with cultural loss and alienation, they can be used to address psychological dysfunction that springs from change and anomie: a major malady facing indigenous people, ethnic groups, and traditional enclaves.

Many other therapeutic methods can be adjusted to serve indigenous, ethnic, and traditional people. Doing so can provide a wealth of techniques for combating the pain, suffering, and dysfunction triggered by outside intrusion, cultural losses, and anomie.

FINAL WORDS

A key goal of this monograph is to develop an understanding of anomie and its power over people. First popularized by Emile Durkheim in the late 19th century, anomie refers to a form of alienation and discomfort that people experience when their way of life is rapidly undercut by forces they cannot control. Durkheim's analysis centered upon rural and ethnic enclaves beset with change that were caused by contact with the modern, outside world. In other words, the original conceptualization of anomie deals with the hurtful impacts of economic and social development upon distinctive, hinterland peoples.

As time went on, the concept of anomie was expanded and broadened by sociologists such as Robert Merton, who depict anomie as arising when people are unable to achieve socially acceptable goals in socially acceptable ways. Merton went on to offer a range of options available to people who find themselves in this sort of stressful situation. The available responses range from apathy and withdrawal, on the one hand, to systematically breaking some or all of the rules of society in order to successfully adapt, on the other. Some of these reactions can emerge as helpful and productive while others are hurtful and negative. The concept of anomie, therefore, is ideally suited for the task of analyzing the disruption caused by social and economic change as well as understanding how people respond in both positive and negative ways.

Having introduced and discussed the importance of anomie, specific applications were analyzed in order to demonstrate how this theory can be employed in a variety of circumstances. Initially, discussions merely expanded the analysis of anomie as presented by Durkheim, Merton, and others in order to more fully recognize its implications and applicability. This led to a consideration of how specific traditional cultures have broken down due to the stress of outside forces, as contrasted with situations where people and their cultures adapted in positive ways.

A specific school of thought, Terror Management Theory, explores how a fear of death can cause people to identify with something that is more immortal than they are. In many cases, their culture or tradition fills that role, providing people with comfort in the belief that their heritage will live on after they die. If the culture to which people identify declines or becomes vulnerable, however, this feeling of permanence and immorality can weaken, leading to increased anxiety and psychological dysfunction.

Currently, the interest in economic development and indigenous cultures is growing. Numerous Native and ethnic studies programs throughout the academic world, for example, seek to address the pain and disruption triggered by outside forces (and their influences) that bring change. Most observers recognize that the agendas of development, even when positive, are often associated with a rapid increase in psychological dysfunction. The work of Harold Napoleon was discussed as an example of this thinking. He argues that alienation and disruption triggered by social change can cause a society-wide pattern of psychological dysfunction, suicide, and other hurtful responses. This is often true even if the changes can be ranked as "beneficial" when evaluated according to the "social indicators" analysis so often employed by evaluators.

Section 3 continued this chain of thought by examining specific tools and tactics. Chapter 9 provided an overview of general concepts while Chapter 10 dealt with two models and tactics that were presented as representative of other available options. The basic message is that cultural sensitivity is an important aspect of dealing with distinctive people who face social and economic change. If appropriate cultural awareness is present, psychological dysfunction, triggered by social and economic change, can be more effectively addressed. I hope this monograph has been useful in that regard.

INDEX

Note: **Bold** page numbers refer to tables and *italic* page numbers refer to figures.

3 Es model ("events," "experience," and "effect") 81, **82**

Achebe, C. 28–30, 37–38, 51, 52, 70
action stage 119, 120, **121**
acute PTSD 77
Adverse Childhood Experiences (ACE) 80
Alaska: Western goods 81; Yup'ik of 38, 41–42, 78
Alcoholics Anonymous (AA) 113–114, 119, 120
ambivalence 125, 126, **127**
American Psychological Association 93
anomie 12–14, **145**; Achebe, Chiuna 28–30; Cargo Cults 31; Durkheim, Emile 17–18, 22, 47, 62, 75; and dysfunction **53**; Fanon, Frantz 28; Ghost Dance 30; Handsome Lake 40, 41; Iroquois and Yup'ik 42; learned helplessness and **84**; Merton, Robert 18–20, 22, 63–64, 70; Napoleon, Harold 78; Rogers, Carl 122–124, **124**; and strain theory 22, **23**; Terror Management Theory and 98–100, **99**
antithesis 141
anxiety disorders 76
Arrow of God (Achebe) 37
Arts and Crafts movement 7–10, **8**

Bandura, A. 83–85
Bateson, G. 133–138, **135**, 140–144
Battiste, M. 52

Becker, E. 91–93, 97
Black Skin, White Masks (Fanon) 27, 51, 144
Bombay Town Planning Act 11
buffers 94, 98

Cargo Cult 30–32, **32**, 35–36
Cervantes, M. de 139
Chagos Islanders 49, 50
choices and adaptations arise 23
Christianity 38, 140
chronic PTSD 77
client-centered therapy **128**; motivational interviewing 125–127, **127**; Rogers, Carl 122–123, **124**, 125
cognitive approach 93
Cognitive Psychology (Neisser) 93
Cold War 50
conflict causes strain 23
conformity 18, *19*, **20**, 30, 63–66, **65**, **72**, **99**
congruence 123, **124**
Consider the Lilies (Smith) 6
contemplation stage 119–120, **121**
Cooper, J. F. 36–38
Cornplanter 66
crime 7, 13, 20, 21, 24, 62, 63
culture 7, 12, 18, 26, 28–32, 37, 38, 40–42, 47, 48, 50, 52, 59–70, **80**, 81, 90–92, 100, 101, 138, 144; competence 114, 116–119, **118**, 127–128, **128**, 144–145; in conflict 23; differences 24; distinct 22–24; PTSD 78–80, **80**, 87; role of 95–97; safety

114–115, **116**, 118, 127, 128, **128**, 132, 144–145; vulnerability 97–98
cybernetics 133, **135**, 137, 143
Cybernetics, or Control and Communication in the Animal and the Machine (Weiner) 133

Deceit, Desire, and the Novel (Girard) 138–139
Decolonizing Methodologies (Smith) 52
Denial of Death, The (Becker) 91–92
Denzin, N. K. 99
deviance 20–22, 24, 62, 63, 71
Diagnostic and Statistical Manual of Mental Disorders (DSM) 76
dialectics 143
Dickens, C. 6, 7, 13, 14
discrepancies 126
Don Quixote (Cervantes) 138, 139
double bind 135, **135**, 136
Durbin, R. 22
Durkheim, E. 9–14, **10**, 17–18, 20–22, 24, 27–29, 37, 42, 47, 48, 53, 59, 61–63, 72, 75, 79, 98, 150
dysfunction 27–28, 53, **53**, **142**

Enlightenment 7
"events," "experience," and "effect" (3 Es model) 81, **82**

family homeostasis model (Bateson) 134–136, **135**
Fanon, F. 27, 28, 51, 52, 144
feedback loop 133
"folk, work, place" 11
Fourth World 47, 50, 52, 53, **53**
French and Indian War 39
Freud, S. 92, 124, 138, 139
Future Shock (Toffler) 14

Geddes, P. 5, 11, 12
Gemeinschaft 9, 22
Gesellschaft 9
Ghost Dance 30–32, **32**, 35
Girard, R. 112, 133, 137–145, **141**, **142**, **145**
Great American Desert 37
Greenberg, J. 93–96

Halloran, M. J. 97
Handsome Lake 40–42, 66, 67
HelpGuide.org 77
Henderson, J. 52
Henry IV Part 1 (Shakespeare) 76
Highland Clearance 6
homeostasis: model 136–137, **137**, 144–145; theory 133–136, **135**, **145**
homogeneity 21

Hubbard, E. 7–9
human nature 7, 138, 144

ideal self 123
imitation 139, 140, **141**, 143
immortality project 92
incongruence 123, **124**, 128
indigenous people 22, 27–31, 36, 38, 41, 47–52, **53**, 78, 81, 86, 97, 101, 114, 115, 133
Industrial Revolution 5–7
innovation 5, 18, *19*, **20**, 40, 41, 63, 66–67, **67**, **72**, 81, 123, 144
innovative manner 21
Iroquois, renaissance 38–41
Ishi 91
Ishi: The Last of his Tribe (Kroeber) 91

Kierkegaard, S. 92
Kirmayer, L. J. 116–117
Kroeber, T. 91

learned helplessness 82–83, **84**
Life Stressor Checklist 81, **82**

mainstream people 62
mainstream population 47
maintenance stage 120, **121**
Maslow, A. 93, 122
mechanical societies 9
megamachines 12
mental structuralism 138, 143, 144
Merton, R. 18–22, 24, 28–30, 40, 42, 53, 59, 62–64, 66, 69–72, 96, 98, 106, 123, 150
Merton's typology 71
Miller, W. R. 125
mimesis 112, 139, 140, **141**, 142–144, 148
mimetic response **142**
Morris, W. 7–9
mortality salience 94–96, 98, 100, 101
motivational Interviewing (MI) 111, 114, 125–127, **127**, **128**
Mumford, L. 11, 12

Napoleon, H. 41–42, 78–80, 83, 84, 86, 151
Narroll, R. 139
Native people (capital N) 47, 48, 51, 52, **53**
native people (lowercase n) 47
Neisser, U. 93
News From Nowhere (Morris) 7
No Longer at Ease (Achebe) 29, 37, 70
non-confrontational 126

Oliver Twist (Dickens) 6, 13
Operant Conditioning 82

154 Index

orderly transition strategy 101, **102**
organic analogy 62
organic societies 10

pain 27–28
pain and uncertainty lead to dysfunction 23
phrenology 143
The Pioneers (Cooper) 36
population 47–48
post-traumatic stress disorder (PTSD) 42,
    76–78, **77**; cultural 78–80, **80**, 87; effect
    81; issues 81–82; learned helplessness
    82–83, **84**, 86–87; self-efficacy 83–87, **85**,
    87; trauma and **82**, 87, **87**
The Prairie (Cooper) 37
precontemplation stage 119, **121**
preparation stage 120, **121**
Pre-Raphaelites 7
preserve heritage strategy 100, **102**
Prochaska, J. O. 119
progressive scapegoat **142**
Protecting Indigenous Knowledge and Heritage:
    A Global Challenge (Battiste and
    Henderson) 52
psychological dysfunction 21
PTSD *see* post-traumatic stress disorder
    (PTSD)
Pyscznski, T. 93

Rank, O. 92
real self 123
rebellion 18, 19, *19*, **20**, 21, 31, 63, 64,
    69–71, **71**, **72**
reconciliation **142**, 143
reference group 70
relapse stage 120, **121**
replace heritage strategy 101, **102**
retreatism 18, 19, *19*, **20**, 21, 41, 42, 63, 64,
    69, 69–70, **72**
Revolutionary War (1776–1783) 39
ritualism *19*
ritualization 18, 19, **20**, 21, 63–64, 67–68,
    68, **72**
Rogers, C. 114, 122–125, **124**, 128, **128**
Rollnick, S. 125
Romanticism 7, 9, 10

Sablonniere, R. 96, 97
Salzman, M. B. 96, 97
scapegoating 139, 140, **141**, 143, 145
self-actualization 122, 123, **124**
self-efficacy 83–87, **85**, **87**
self-esteem 94–98, 100
self-help program 113–114

Seligman, M. 83
semi-directed method 125, 126, **127**
Seven Years War 39
shell shock 76, 79
Skinner, B. F. 82–83
Smith, L. C. 6
Smith, L. T. 52
social dysfunction 21
social structuralism 9, 10, 18, 22, 24, 138,
    143, 144
social theory 8–11
social workers 43
soldier's heart (PTSD) 76; *see also* post-
    traumatic stress disorder (PTSD)
Solomon, S. 93
"speaking in tongues" 117
Stages of Change model 119–122, **121**,
    125–126, 128, **128**
Steven, M. 83
strain causes pain and uncertainty 23
strain theory 20–22, 24, 28, 29, 31
strategic planners 43
stressor-related disorders 76
structuralism, mental 138
subgroups 62
Substance Abuse and Mental Health
    Services Administration of the United
    States (SAMHSA) 76, 80, 81
synthesis 42–43, 141

Teaching Cultural Competence in Health Care:
    A Review of Current Concepts, Policies and
    Practices 118
technics 12
Technics and Civilization (Mumford) 12
termination stage 120, **121**
Terror Management Theory (TMT)
    90–94; and anomie 98–100, **99**; Becker,
    Ernest 91–93, 97; cultural vulnerability
    97–98; culture, role of 95–97; heritage,
    preserving and replacing 100, 101, **102**;
    mortality salience 94; orderly transition
    101, **102**; self-esteem 94–95
therapists 43
thesis 141
Things Fall Apart (Achebe) 28, 29, 37
Third World 28, 47, 50–53, **53**
TMT *see* Terror Management Theory
    (TMT)
Toffler, A. 14
Tönnies, F. 9–12, **10**
Towards a Culturally Competent System of
    Care (Cross, Bazron, Dennis and Isaacs)
    117–118

traditional people 8, 18, 22, 26, 32, 47, 48, 50–53, **53**, 101, 103, 114, 119, 122, 123, 125–128, 133, 142–145
traditional scapegoat **142**
Transtheoretical Model 119
trauma **82**, **87**; cultural 75–87
triangulation 98–99

Usborne, E. 96, 97

Velicer, W. F. 119
Vietnam War 76
Violence and the Sacred (Girard) 139

Walden 2 (Skinner) 82–83
Wallace, A. 39–40
Walle, Alf H. 97
The Way of Being Human (Napoleon) 41
Webb, E. J. 99
Weiner, N. 133
Wolfe, T. 14
Wretched of the Earth (Fanon) 27

You Can't Go Home Again (Wolfe) 14
Youngblood, J. 52
Yup'ik 32, 38, 41–43, 78, 79, 83, 84

Zola, E. 143

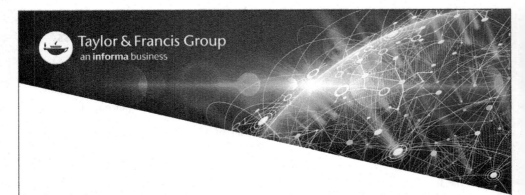

Taylor & Francis eBooks

www.taylorfrancis.com

A single destination for eBooks from Taylor & Francis with increased functionality and an improved user experience to meet the needs of our customers.

90,000+ eBooks of award-winning academic content in Humanities, Social Science, Science, Technology, Engineering, and Medical written by a global network of editors and authors.

TAYLOR & FRANCIS EBOOKS OFFERS:

- A streamlined experience for our library customers
- A single point of discovery for all of our eBook content
- Improved search and discovery of content at both book and chapter level

REQUEST A FREE TRIAL
support@taylorfrancis.com